PARLIAMENTARY RESEARCHER

HOW TO BE A PARLIAMENTARY RESEARCHER

Robert Dale

First published in Great Britain in 2015 by
Biteback Publishing Ltd
Westminster Tower
3 Albert Embankment
London SE1 7SP

ISBN 978-1-84954-930-1

10 9 8 7 6 5 4 3 2 1

A CIP catalogue record for this book is available from the British Library.

Set in Quadraat

Printed and bound in Great Britain by
CPI Group (UK) Ltd, Croydon CR0 4YY

Contents

Foreword

BY MR SPEAKER

MUCH IS WRITTEN about the work of MPs, but comparatively less is written about their staff. They are a 3,000-strong army of parliamentary researchers, caseworkers, office managers and secretaries who support MPs in their parliamentary and constituency duties. They are the unsung heroes of the Westminster Village. This book, the first of its kind to be written by a parliamentary researcher, underlines this statement and illustrates the important role that staff play in our Parliament.

To serve a community as its MP is a great privilege – and an even greater responsibility. Being an MP is a unique job in many ways, perhaps most acutely felt by the absence of a formal job description; both a blessing and a curse for those learning how best to support them. While MPs have the freedom and flexibility to manage their office and staffing arrangements in a manner that best suits their needs and that of their constituents, it also means that no two MPs' offices are the same. The office manager of one MP may find that upon moving to work in the same role for his or her colleague, the responsibilities bear little resemblance to those previously held. Additionally, the scope of the role of MP continues to evolve over time.

Since I first became an MP in 1997, the most perceptible change has been the positive impact that technology has had on my ability to communicate with constituents. The rise in the proportion of casework that can now reach me by post, email and social media has proven that technology has reformed traditional ways of working and engaging with constituents. The changes in technology have also had an impact on the ability of the public and press to scrutinise a Member of Parliament's work, resulting in much greater transparency and accountability.

This step change in the responsibilities of MPs also requires that those working for an MP are equally flexible and dynamic. It is vital to the work of MPs that their staff are hard-working, bright and dedicated and can support them to serve their electorate as effectively as possible and I believe it is important that people of ability and commitment, whatever their background, are given equal opportunity to work for a Member of Parliament. I am pleased to see this book asserting the value of recent initiatives such as the Speaker's Parliamentary Placement Scheme – which I am proud to support – and the Parliamentary Academy Scheme, which are both opening up access to Parliament.

There are thousands of people who support our democracy, from the parliamentary officials who run the parliamentary estate to the civil servants who support ministerial offices, to MPs' staff. It is this rich network that ensures our democracy can function and that the public are represented. MPs are only one cog in a very large wheel. Without staff, MPs would be without the vital briefings, research, advice and mental support necessary to scrutinise legislation, engage with their electorate and stand up for the needs of their local area.

My thoughts on this matter are not merely the consequence of observation. I myself started my time at Westminster working part time as a researcher to Dr Michael Clark MP. I remember on my first day walking through Central Lobby and experiencing the intense sense of awe that everybody – MPs and staffers alike – feels on their first day. It was an immense privilege to work for a Member of Parliament and to feel that I was playing a (admittedly) small part in our democracy. I have to say that, even so many years later and inhabiting a different role, that feeling has not gone away. I know that there are many other MPs with similar life stories, but also a large number of colleagues who will walk through Central Lobby upon being elected a Member of Parliament for the first time.

I believe that more can be done to improve the working experiences of parliamentary staffers. All jobs present their own unique challenges, and working in Westminster is no exception. It can be difficult and at times will inevitably be stressful. Historically, there has been no gentle learning curve. Instead, working for a Member of Parliament was a test of courage from day one. On the morning of their first day, staffers could well find themselves undertaking an important task for which they have no previous experience or training, such as tabling Parliamentary Questions, briefing an MP for a TV interview, writing a letter to a secretary of state on behalf of a constituent, or trying to talk their employer down from an idea that is likely to result in cold stares from senior colleagues for the foreseeable future. MPs employ their staff directly, and so while it is for each MP and their political parties to manage staff employment, the House of Commons Service recognises the importance of supporting their learning and development. Back when I was a junior member of staff – and, indeed, more recently – new parliamentary researchers were more or less handed a key to their office and told to get on with it. The difficulty is, of course, that as no two MPs – even MPs from the same party or adjoining constituencies – are alike, the responsibilities of staff vary widely as a consequence. However, there is now training available which provides assistance for caseworkers and researchers on topical issues likely to affect a large number of parliamentary colleagues' constituents, as well as introductory sessions for new staffers. The days when 'staff induction' meant trying not to get lost between the Aye Lobby and the toilets in Central Lobby are, happily, behind us, yet I remain conscious that there are still areas that we could improve on in order that members' staff are fully equipped to assist their MP in his or her duties.

It is important that staff are able to provide support for their MP. It is equally important that the House provides support for MPs' staff. In 2014, I established a confidential helpline for parliamentary staff as an additional measure to help them identify where to go for guidance on areas such as employment conditions, bullying and harassment, personal problems or any other issues that might affect their work, health or general wellbeing. These steps, along with the diversity and inclusion initiatives such as the Workplace Equality Networks and the House of Commons Nursery, both of which are open to MPs' staff, are steps in the right direction to modernise the culture of the House of Commons and to ensure that it is a 21st-century organisation.

The importance of parliamentary staffers looks set to continue to grow over this parliament. The 2015 report of the Speaker's Commission on Digital Democracy set targets for the Commons to be delivered in the next five years, in order to ensure that everyone understands what the House does. These targets include a commitment to making Parliament fully interactive and digital, and creating a new forum for public participation in the debating function of the House of Commons. Staffers will be at the forefront of assisting MPs and the House if we are to meet these recommendations.

It has long been the frustration of staffers that none of their previous colleagues has written a comprehensive guide exploring the key tasks, expectations and duties that they are expected to fulfil – until now, that is. *How to Be a Parliamentary Researcher* is a hugely important resource that will benefit not only our current and future staffers, but MPs as well. This book is filled with the theoretical and practical guidance necessary to help demystify Parliament and make it more accessible to anyone who aspires to work at the heart of our vibrant democracy.

Rt Hon. John Bercow MP
Member of Parliament for Buckingham and
Speaker of the House of Commons
June 2015

Introductions

I'VE WORKED FOR MPs in Parliament and the constituency, so when I was elected I had a good idea of the kind of team I wanted. Arriving mid-way through a parliament, we needed to hit the ground running.

Robert Dale worked with me in my previous job. He had no experience of Parliament but I knew he would be loyal, entrepreneurial in the role and learn quickly how to be a parliamentary researcher. We walked into Parliament together and, from the first day to the last, we were a team. Rob became, in my biased opinion, the best parliamentary researcher an MP could wish to have at their side. From running the Westminster office, to supporting my response to a government Bill, showing my constituents around the parliamentary estate and representing me to journalists, I knew I could trust Rob, no matter what the task, to get it done to an impressively high standard.

Rob and I share a passion for digital technology and social media. Working together, we pushed at every opportunity to introduce new ideas and ways of working to improve levels of engagement with the electorate. We crowd-sourced speeches, produced a fantastic e-newsletter and ran surveys that interacted with thousands of people. I'm pleased to see Rob highlight throughout this book the important role digital communication will play in Parliament in the future.

An MP relies massively on the support, talents and dedication of their staffers. My team in the constituency were brilliant too. Alan, Lynsey, Colleen and Ian worked hard every day and provided a service that helped thousands of people in Corby and East Northamptonshire. We learnt the hard way that, in an ultra-marginal seat, even with a good local reputation, you can't hold back a national swing, but we are very proud of the work we did together.

There is no official training service or manual for new staffers. For parliamentary researchers this is made worse by the fact that many of them are an MP's only member of staff in Westminster. That is why this book is so important. It is full of insider knowledge, innovative ideas and practical advice that any current or aspiring parliamentary researcher should read and absorb.

Andy Sawford
MP for Corby and East Northamptonshire 2012–15

• • •

I HAD A very special two and a half years in Parliament. My first day as a parliamentary researcher, Monday 19 November 2012, began by walking through the public entrance of Portcullis House at the side of my newly elected boss, Andy Sawford, who had just won Labour's first by-election gain from the Conservatives in seventeen years.

Andy and I were met by one of the House's top officials, taken along the 'Bobby Kennedy' route through the underbelly of the parliamentary estate (it's called the 'Bobby Kennedy route' because it takes you through the Portcullis House kitchens in a scene very similar to where the candidate for the Democrat presidential nomination was assassinated) to the Pass Office where we collected our official 'passholder' accreditation.

From there, we went for a short meeting with the then Clerk of the House of Commons, Sir Robert Rogers, and next to the Whips' Office to be welcomed into the Parliamentary Labour Party. That afternoon, we were joined by some of the most loyal and active members of the by-election campaign. Together we sat in the special gallery above the Commons chamber and watched as Andy was sworn in to become the Member of Parliament for Corby and East Northamptonshire.

My final day in the role ended at 6 a.m. on Friday 8 May 2015 as I, along with Andy's friends, family and local party members, fought back the tears and applauded him as he drove out of the Lodge Park Sports Centre car park, where the general election count had just taken place. We were optimistic going into the count and the national polls looked good for us, but we knew it would be close. Unfortunately, despite all our best efforts, the electorate swung away from us and our long-term aspirations came to an abrupt end.

In the time between these two dates, I saw an MP's office develop from nothing to become an organisation that helped over 6,000 constituents. In Parliament, Andy went from a rookie backbencher to a highly regarded shadow minister. He led the opposition's response to a government Bill and introduced three significant Private Members' Bills of his own – on zero-hours contracts, strengthening the Gangmasters Licensing Authority and permitting a public rail operator. Working together, Andy, myself and the constituency staffers created an engaging digital presence and an e-newsletter with one of the highest subscriber rates of any MP, and nurtured an excellent relationship with our local media.

Most importantly, we worked hard every day to earn the trust of the electorate and demonstrate that not all MPs are the same.

I didn't study politics at college or university; the language and processes of Parliament were a completely new language and culture to me. Fortunately, the by-election that brought Andy to the Commons was so high profile that most MPs and their parliamentary researchers had been drafted to visit the constituency at some point to help. This was the perfect icebreaker and meant I could approach most people, strike up a conversation and ask for their advice as I tried to learn the ropes.

Even on the first day Andy was receiving messages from constituents asking for his help with various casework issues. As I was his only member of staff for the first few weeks I had to quickly find a way of responding to these people and assisting Andy in taking up their cases. In those early days I spent a great amount of time knocking on the doors of neighbouring MPs' offices to seek the advice of their staff.

At the same time, we were trying to organise a permanent office in the parliamentary estate, set up email and phone accounts, order stationery, find and open a constituency office, employ an office manager and caseworker to work in it, arrange help and advice surgeries and visits to local schools and businesses, meet with journalists and, of course, hit the ground running inside the Commons.

There is no guide or official induction for these first few weeks. After the welcome meetings with the clerk and the whips, new MPs – and their parliamentary researcher if they have one at this early stage – are, mostly, left to find their feet and fight for their place. As one former parliamentary researcher says, 'Your first few days in Westminster are sink or swim.' We were fortunate – at least we were given a temporary office at the beginning. Spare a thought for the new MPs after each general election who spend their first month hot-desking across the different canteens within the parliamentary estate. Kate Green, elected MP for Stretford and Urmston in 2010, said, 'In thirty years of working life, I have never found myself in such an alien working environment. Not having an office for the first several weeks left me totally disoriented, unable to focus on getting to grips with the job, and very stressed.'[1]

While all this meant those early weeks were tough and exhausting for Andy and me, they were hugely exciting too. Each day brought new challenges, new places inside Parliament to find, new people to meet and new things to learn about the ways and workings of the Palace of Westminster.

As Mr Speaker points out in his foreword, every MP is different, and so too is the set-up of their staff. This means there isn't a definitive template for how a parliamentary researcher should do their job. It is for the MP to set the tone for where they want their staffers' focus and priorities to be – building their media profile, writing speeches, tabling Questions, responding to constituents' emails or giving them tours of Parliament, finding out the latest gossip going round the staff bar or running their social media accounts. In reality, the job of the parliamentary researcher is to do a bit of all of these tasks, always and constantly.

With these roles comes great responsibility. The majority of MPs will have worked hard for many years, sacrificed a lot of time with their family and spent a significant amount of money to be elected. They then must hand over huge amounts of their life to their staffers, who will run their diary, guide them on what to say and take actions on their behalf with thousands of constituents, journalists, businesses and charities.

Anyone who works for an MP, either in Parliament or in the constituency office, should be hugely proud of the work they do. Looking at each day individually, it may not seem like much is

---

1 Written evidence submitted by Kate Green MP to the Administration Committee in January 2013 for their inquiry, *First weeks at Westminster: induction arrangements for new MPs in 2015* http://www.publications.parliament.uk/pa/cm201314/cmselect/cmadmin/193/193we09.htm

achieved – indeed, a good day is often judged to be so if you leave the office no further behind on work than you were when you walked in that morning.

But take a step back and look at things in the longer term. Across the country, staffers are connecting hundreds of thousands of people with their MP in a way that has never happened before. Whether it's dealing with casework or organising a jobs fair, responding to waves of policy-lobbying campaign emails or running an MP's Facebook page, staffers are playing a hugely important role in taking the MP from being a distant figure in the Commons to one that constituents can know, follow and feel engaged with.

I had the privilege of working for a boss that valued his staff and cared for us. I believe we, in response to this, showed the loyalty and commitment an MP needs in order to focus on best serving their constituents. Unfortunately, as Chapter 3 of this book will demonstrate, not all MPs are great team leaders. We must therefore support Mr Speaker and the Parliament authorities to take the necessary action to end the abuse and exploitation some staffers face, particularly because, for most parliamentary researchers, this will be their first real job after graduating from university. We must also reform the staffing system to give the public greater trust in it, for example by increasing transparency of who staffers are and what roles they perform.

This book is the first to be written about the huge array of tasks parliamentary researchers carry out. Sixty years ago Members of Parliament had no staff; now they collectively employ nearly 3,000 people. This book explores the context behind this transformation and provides a guide for each task a parliamentary researcher will perform. Crucially, it looks ahead to the important role they will play as the House of Commons adopts a 'digital-by-default' outlook and members of the public demand greater openness and accountability from their representatives.

I have attempted to pick out key insights and experiences from my time working for Andy Sawford MP. I've also drawn upon the best ideas from my network of friends and colleagues inside Parliament. Similarly, a parliamentary researcher interacts everyday with many different outside organisations – charities, businesses, lobbyists, think tanks, pressure groups and, of course, constituents. To demonstrate how a parliamentary researcher can work successfully with these bodies and individuals, this book includes several contributions from some of the leaders in their field. Finally, I personally believe the role that technology has to play in an MP's operations is an issue that is not focused on enough. This book therefore carries an emphasis on 'digital' throughout.

It is my aim that, by bringing together theory and practice in this way, *How to Be a Parliamentary Researcher* creates a blueprint of how to succeed when working inside an MP's Westminster office.

Robert Dale
July 2015

Chapter 1

The rise of the parliamentary staffer

SEVENTY-EIGHT PER CENT of the total amount that Members of Parliament claim in expenses goes on the employment of staffers. Between them, it is the job of office managers, caseworkers, secretaries and parliamentary researchers to do the ugly work so that their boss can focus on his or her main job: performing. The Speaker of the House of Commons, John Bercow MP (who began his time in Westminster as a part-time researcher for Dr Michael Clark MP) calls staffers the 'unsung heroes of the Westminster Village'. The volume of work for today's MP can be immense and the demands and expectations are so great that it would be nearly impossible for them to perform at the levels the public expects without this small team of dedicated people working for them.

The role of the parliamentary staffer, though, is a relatively recent addition to the House of Commons. In 1969, just over 700 years on from Simon de Montfort's first ever parliament, which sat in the grand Westminster Hall – the only part of the parliamentary estate to have survived both the Great Fire of 1834 and the Luftwaffe's bombing during the Second World War – the Commons voted for a motion that granted 'payment to Members of this House of an allowance in respect of expenses incurred for their parliamentary duties on secretarial assistance within a maximum of £500 for the first twelve months'.[2] Today, the expenses system has expanded and MPs are granted £140,000 a year to use for the employment of staff, a figure calculated to enable each member to employ the equivalent of four or five people full time.

The rise of the parliamentary staffer has, then, been sudden and significant – so much so that in 2001 the parliamentary estate opened a whole new building to help accommodate the growing number of staff working for MPs in Westminster. Portcullis House, a state-of-the-art office block for over 200 MPs, and which came in at a whopping £235 million price tag to the taxpayer (equivalent to over £1 million per office), can in some ways be viewed as a physical expression of the growing importance and influence of parliamentary staffers within the Westminster Village.

The need for an MP to have staffers has grown in response to three key external pressures, which have forced extensions upon the role an MP is expected to fulfil. These are: an increase in the workload of an MP; the development of digital technology; and the public's demand for greater openness and accountability.

Trust in MPs had been falling for many years, but the expenses scandal of 2009 sent it plummeting to previously unimaginable depths – with further cash for access and cash for questions

---

2 Hansard, 18 December 1969, Members (Expenses and Allowances) hansard.millbanksystems.com/commons/1969/dec/18/members-expenses-and-allowances#column_1693

scandals since preventing the Commons from rebuilding its reputation with the general public. Each year the Hansard Society conduct their *Audit of Political Engagement* that provides 'a health check on our democratic system'. In 2004, the society found that 36 per cent of people were satisfied with Parliament; by 2012, this had dropped to 23 per cent. It is often said that the only people the public distrust more than MPs are bankers and estate agents, but polling carried out by Ipsos MORI in 2014 found that the public actually trusted bankers nearly twice as much as they did politicians. Of the 1,116 people interviewed in their *Trust in Professions* study, only 16 per cent said they 'trust politicians to tell the truth'. There is, though, some hope for MPs. When the Hansard Society changed their question to ask people how well they thought their *local* MP was doing his or her job, 34 per cent in 2012 said they were satisfied, a rating nearly 50 per cent higher than for MPs in general.

Against a tide of public anger, apathy and frustration with Westminster and national party politics, many MPs have made the decision to work harder locally. This has meant giving more priority and greater focus to constituency issues and delivering the best possible service they can to their voters. Roy Hattersley, a former deputy leader of the Labour Party, summarises that there is now an 'increasing belief that the balance of MPs' time and work should tilt heavily towards their constituencies'.[3] In practice, this means 'the MP is expected to be on the spot',[4] visiting and supporting local schools, businesses and charities, raising issues in Parliament or lobbying government ministers on their behalf, or leading or joining local campaigns on matters such as an ambulance station closure, cuts to street lighting or problems with potholes. Campaign literature, both online and in print, produced by candidates and MPs seeking re-election at the 2015 general election

3 'Ideology's our life, Esther', Roy Hattersley, *The Guardian*, 31 July 2009

4 Robert Rogers and Rhodri Walters, *How Parliament Works*, 6th edition (Routledge, 2006), p. 118

was notable for its focus on the personal and local, rather than the national party and Westminster politics. Many chose to highlight any family connections they had with the area, emphasise their record of activity in the constituency and make personal, tangible pledges, such as to be a 'full-time MP' and to be transparent about their expenses.

As well as getting stuck into local campaigns and being more accountable, the electorate expect their MP to travel across the constituency to hold help and advice surgeries and take up individual pieces of casework (usually a personal issue in someone's life for which they want help from the MP to resolve). Casework has become 'the determining influence upon the great majority of MPs'[5] believes Sir Robert Rogers, the former Clerk of the House of Commons.

Casework can cover almost any and every issue imaginable – from helping a constituent get their children into a particular school, sorting problems with social services, taking on a rogue landlord or intervening in a dispute between two neighbours. Constituents also attend help and advice surgeries to raise concerns about levels of dog fouling, the state of the flower beds in the town or to complain that their post arrives too late in the day. Following one help and advice surgery in 2013, Karen Buck MP listed on Twitter some of the issues her constituents had been asking for help on: 'Getting M&S to change a pair of trousers. Help with paying for a wedding. Neighbour who didn't look after friend's cat during holiday.'[6]

Isabel Hardman of *The Spectator* has looked into some of the most comical examples of casework. Hardman found that Grant Shapps MP was called by a constituent who wanted him to help load and unload their removal van as they moved house; Alun

---

5 Ibid., p. 119

6 www.twitter.com/KarenPBuckMP, 12 July 2013

Cairns MP was asked to arrange for a constituent's dog to be fed; David Burrowes MP had to sort out a dead pigeon that a constituent had spotted on the top of a bus shelter; Therese Coffey MP was asked if she could recommend a good dating agency; while Tim Loughton MP 'was left at a loss when he was asked by one local for advice on how to make the man who had dumped her change his mind about their affair'.[7] As Hardman concludes: 'Casework is a bit like 999 calls, some is very serious, some is not always fully sensible.'

The MP is expected to pursue all these matters without fear or favour ceaselessly until the best possible outcome for the constituent has been reached (it is not uncommon for an MP to send upwards of fifty letters over the course of a parliament on behalf of just one constituent). In some of the more deprived areas of the country, such as inner east London, Newcastle or Liverpool, the MP will probably employ more than one caseworker in order to try to meet demand on these services, and may spend more time themselves signing letters, making calls, talking through the issues with their staff or meeting with constituents than they do sitting in the House of Commons. Indeed, research carried out by Young Legal Aid Lawyers in 2012 found that for a third of MPs, casework took up 'between 50 and 74 per cent of their time'.[8]

Most MPs dutifully accept this growing aspect of their role and regard it as a key part of their democratic responsibilities. A former parliamentary researcher to a government minister says, 'Casework is the most important job in an MP's office. Earning a good reputation through word of mouth as a hardworking local MP counts for more at the ballot box than ministerial cars and appearing on *Newsnight*.' However, some disagree with the changing balance

---

7 See http://blogs.spectator.co.uk/coffeehouse/2013/08/the-silly-season-that-never-stops-the-weird-demands-from-constituents-to-their-mps

8 *Nowhere else to turn: The impact of legal aid cuts on MPs' ability to help their constituents.* Young Legal Aid Lawyers http://www.younglegalaidlawyers.org/sites/default/files/YLAL_Nowhere_else_to_turn.pdf

of priorities. Roy Hattersley, after noting MPs' growing focus on constituency and casework issues, believes that this has acted to 'discredit politics and diminish politicians ... an MP's job is politics', he says, not to be a social worker.

The second external pressure that has forced changes to the role of an MP has been the evolution of digital technology. New forms of communication are rewriting and re-creating the way in which people want to connect with their MP. As David Plouffe, manager of the 2008 Obama for America campaign, says, 'So many people are living their lives through technology – how can we expect their interactions with politics to be the one exception?'[9]

Millions of people are participating in politics through sites like 38 Degrees, Change.org and even the government's e-petitions site. Similarly, as this book will show, hundreds of charities and pressure groups are mobilising their members and supporters to lobby MPs to support their campaign, sign Early Day Motions (EDMs), ask Questions in the House or attend a mass lobby in Central Lobby. That these campaigns can be successful in changing legislation illustrates the new expectations the public have of their MP. No longer do they vote them off to Westminster once every five years and leave them to it. Now, constituents want to be able to share their views and influence their MP throughout the year. The 2010–15 group of MPs are widely considered to have been the most rebellious bunch ever. Part of the reason for this may be the pressure constituents were able to apply on their local MP to be a mouthpiece for their constituents and constituency first, and a member of a political party second.

One member, elected before the invention of email, recalls that he used to receive as few as eight letters a week. All of this correspondence could be responded to during a Sunday afternoon, enabling him to be free for the rest of the week to focus on parliamentary business.

---

9 David Plouffe, *The Audacity to Win* (New York: Viking/The Penguin Group, 2009), p. 21

Today, MPs have their inboxes filled with hundreds of emails every day from a mixture of constituents wanting help or lobbying them to vote for or against an upcoming motion in the Commons, as well as various charities, businesses, think tanks and pressure groups asking them for a meeting or to support their latest campaign. On top of this, they'll be receiving numerous communications from the party's headquarters, setting out the key messages and talking points for that day. Mel Stride, Conservative MP for Central Devon, estimates that all of this adds up to '3,000 pieces of correspondence a month'.[10] This is far too much information for even the most organised person to deal with on their own.

More recently, social media has further diversified the channels through which constituents expect to be able to communicate with their MP. At the beginning of 2010, just 111 MPs were on Twitter; now that figure has risen to around 500. Later in this book, Steve Hatch, Facebook's UK & Ireland director, says that through social media 'leaders and decision-makers are connecting directly to people'. Social media has added significantly to an MP's ability to transform him or herself from a distant figure in the Commons to a person who constituents can know, follow and feel engaged with. Facebook, for example, has created a special Q&A function for MPs to run online surgeries or discuss local campaigns and planning issues with constituents, as well as a dedicated 'Mentions' app to help them manage their accounts more easily while on the go.

We can look across the Atlantic for inspiration in how to use these tools. In 2010, as a heavy snowstorm battered New Jersey on the east coast of the United States, the city's mayor, Cory Booker, live-tweeted his activities as he and his staff drove around clearing driveways, delivering nappies and organising where to send the snow ploughs. By doing so, he turned his Twitter feed into a public service tool – responding live to the requests of his

10 'Words from Westminster: wading through an MP's inbox', *Mid Devon Gazette*, 27 January 2015

electorate. *Time* reported that one resident posted about Booker: 'He's like a superhero with a shovel.'[11] US politicians are also more advanced in using newer forms of social media. The 2016 Republican presidential nominee candidate Bobby Jindal used Instagram to communicate an 'official behind the scenes look' at his 'life and journey on the campaign trail'. Similarly, his fellow Republican opponent Rand Paul announced (on his Facebook page) 'Did you hear? I joined @Snapchat! For daily updates & behind-the-scenes footage follow: senatorrandpaul on the photo sharing app. I'm sending my first snap tonight'.[12]

The United States have a term called the 'sophomore surge'. When applied in the UK, it suggests that a modern MP will typically receive a small increase in votes the first time they are up for re-election. This is because these politicians, such as Booker, Jindal and Rand, tend to be better at using their energy and resources (and staffers) to run personal, rather than party, campaigns. As Douglas Carswell, UKIP's only MP and author of the book *The end of politics and the birth of iDemocracy*, has put it, 'politics is being repersonalised'. Carswell describes how:

> Rather than try to coax and encourage a news editor to carry the message I want to the voter, I am able to cut out the middleman and the medium, and communicate directly. And the communication becomes a two-way process. The internet allows the voter to put the direct questions and pressure on lawmakers.
>
> This niche, direct communication enables voters to do something they've been unable to do for generations: make a choice of whom to vote for in terms of the personality and calibre of the candidate, rather than the quality of the party brand.[13]

---

11 See http://content.time.com/time/nation/article/0,8599,2039945,00.html

12 See www.facebook.com/RandPaul/posts/10152022425591107

13 Douglas Carswell MP, *The end of politics and the birth of iDemocracy* (London: Biteback Publishing, 2012), p. 187

Technology and social media aren't an end in themselves. They should be about opening up Parliament to give the public's voice a greater hearing. They should be about explaining the work of MPs and showing why it matters to the communities they represent. They should be about helping people to engage in politics – not necessarily party politics with a capital 'P' – but engaging people in local community issues such as roads being blocked because of snow, or household waste bins that haven't been collected, or personal issues such as their family member's battle with cancer, or a worker's battle with an exploitative zero-hours contracts employer. UK MPs, therefore, shouldn't ignore digital technology, they should embrace it. And whether they like it or not, it's happening. In addition to constituents demanding to engage with their MP through technology, the House of Commons expects it too. The Speaker's Commission on Digital Democracy aims to have a 'fully interactive and digital' Parliament by 2020 and its recommendations for achieving this are fundamentally about public participation, storytelling and direct engagement between politician and elector.

As well as engaging with constituents through social media, you need to be organised across the web in order to pick up on any other attention your MP may receive online.

James Carville, Bill Clinton's 1992 presidential campaign lead strategist, had a famous mantra that 'speed kills', and while an MP's office does not operate at the same intensity as a US presidential candidate's 'War Room', the phrase has relevance for a parliamentary researcher seeking to keep their boss ahead of events. You will want the ability to quickly 'listen in' to the conversations constituents are having with each other online about the area (and sometimes about the MP) and advise your boss to get involved when you think they'll be able to play a useful role. Doing so will demonstrate a genuine passion for the area while allowing you to pick up on local sentiment and opinion of the work your MP is doing and gauge their reputation among the electorate.

Just as constituents expect the MP to travel across the constituency to run surgeries in their town or village, they want their MP to go to them online, and join them in an environment in which they feel most comfortable. These spaces can vary enormously, from a Facebook page to a weekly, hour-long 'hashtag debate' on Twitter, a hyperlocal news website,[14] a petition on Change.org, a group on Streetlife (a 'local social network' focused on individual postcodes that has over 1 million users) or a discussion group on Mumsnet (which has 14 million visits a month). You should therefore carry out an extensive audit of the 'digital ecology' of the constituency to identify these spaces and set up efficient ways to monitor the conversations constituents are having through them. What is key about this local digital ecology though is that it is community-led, and therefore largely free of politics – it should not be your ambition to always lead debates in these spaces or fill them with political messages.

Similarly, an MP will want to know as soon as possible if a news story has been published that mentions them. This is because they will either want to promote this article or blog, such as by posting it on Twitter, sharing it on Facebook or asking a supportive resident to flag it up on a forum. Equally importantly, if the statement made about the MP is inaccurate, untrue or misleading, they will want to get out a rebuttal as quickly as possible before this incorrect version establishes itself as the general consensus.

A prudent MP's office will, therefore, also be set up with Lexis-Nexis and Google Alerts, which will notify staffers whenever a news article or blog post that mentions the MP is published. The

14 The term 'hyperlocal' is given to blogs that are run by members of a community and that post news and information only about the area in which they live

office should also use RSS feeds to allow them to easily keep updated on all other new content being posted on local newspaper websites, hyperlocal blogs, forums, as well as the websites of their political opponents (and influential Westminster commentators).

For the busy MP it is difficult and time-consuming to keep track of the latest developments and trends in digital communications, as well as monitoring all of the forums, Facebook pages and other digital networks their constituents may be using. It is therefore often left to their staffers to nudge and guide them through this new world – for example, many staffers will send out the majority of their boss's tweets and Facebook posts. It is perhaps in this digital work where a parliamentary researcher has the greatest opportunity to flex their skills and grow their influence; mastering how to run an MP's Facebook page, with engaging images and content crafted to encourage voters to 'like' and 'share' with their own network, requires a high level of digital communication and technological skills – skills that many MPs will confess to being desperately short of themselves.

While MPs attempt to respond positively to the growing pressure on their services in the constituency, and adapt to the fast-moving world of digital communications, the electorate also expect them to be busy in Parliament and more accountable and open about their activities there.

An MP must still attend Parliament to vote, speak in debates, table Questions, sign EDMs, pursue Private Members' Bills and sit on select committees. On top of this, many will have ministerial or shadow ministerial roles that add hours of work to their week. In the recent past, few members of the public would have bothered to take the time to follow their local MP's activities in Parliament. Today, the website TheyWorkForYou monitors an MP's every move and neatly ranks them by the number of times they speak in the Commons, how many Questions they table and how they vote on each motion. Other websites like Note My Vote, which allows members of the public to vote on motions before the House of Commons does (and was created by a former parliamentary researcher), and Members Interests, which when installed on a person's laptop turns 'the names of any MPs on the page automatically into clickable links that will take you to an entry in the Register of Members' Interests', demonstrate that the public will continue finding ways of using the internet and open data to impose greater transparency upon MPs.

MPs work long hours to try to fulfil all these duties and expectations. In 2011, the Hansard Society surveyed MPs elected in the previous year's general election.[15] They found:

- The 2010 new intake of MPs initially expected a sixty-hour week (plus travel) but six months on were working a 69-hour week.

- They split their working time 63 per cent in Westminster and 37 per cent in their constituencies – but constituency casework takes up the largest share of their time.

- A vast number reported that long working hours and Westminster/constituency demands have a detrimental effect on their personal and family lives; words such as 'overwhelming', 'devastating' and 'a struggle' were common.

The job of the MP, then, has clearly become much more chaotic since the first introduction of staffers back in 1969. Every activity is posted on the internet and there is no escape from the scrutiny and demands of constituents. Having initially been employed to provide secretarial assistance to an MP, a staffer's role has evolved and grown into one where they seek to provide clarity and control

15 *A Year in the Life: From Member of Public to Member of Parliament, interim briefing paper* (London: Hansard Society, June 2011)

over their MP's activities, and to help them build a deeper and more engaging connection with their electorate. Just as every Olympic athlete will have around them a dedicated team of physios, nutritionists and trainers, for an MP to be at the top of their game they too need a close network of trusted, loyal and skilled staff to keep them on track, focused and performing to the best of their ability.

Chapter 2

In the thick of it?

EACH CONSTITUENCY IS different, as is each Member of Parliament, so there is no official structure to how an MP's office must operate. The Independent Parliamentary Standards Authority (IPSA), which was set up following the 2009 expenses scandal and oversees and regulates MPs' salaries, costs and expenses, has identified seven roles for staffers to fulfil: an office manager; caseworker; senior caseworker; secretary; senior secretary; and parliamentary assistant or senior parliamentary assistant (both these roles are traditionally, and colloquially, known as being a 'researcher'). MPs receive an overall budget of £140,000 to employ staff (London area MPs receive an additional 5 per cent to give them a total available budget of £147,000). These figures are set by the IPSA and should allow an MP to employ at least four full-time members of staff, as well as to cover the lunch and travel expenses for young people on work experience. The role of special advisers (Spads) – who work for Cabinet and shadow Cabinet MPs – sits outside the IPSA guidelines because they are classed as being a political appointment, rather than a parliamentary one. They are therefore not paid for through an MP's parliamentary expenses, but directly by the political party.

IPSA has also allocated each role with specific duties (which are listed in full at the end of this chapter). The parliamentary researcher will be expected, for example, to draft speeches to be delivered in the House of Commons and the caseworker will provide assistance to the MP with casework issues, but the reality of working in such a small team means that most staffers will pitch in and work together across these boundaries. Paul Flynn, the MP for Newport West since 1987 and author of the book *How to Be an MP*, states: 'It's inefficient and disruptive to confine staff to strict silos of work on IPSA lines.' In many offices, a caseworker may well draft part of a speech or a Parliamentary Question that relates to a specific issue they are working on locally. Underlining the growing constituency focus for many MPs, the majority will base most of their staffers in the local office and have only a parliamentary researcher, and possibly an intern, running the operation in Westminster.

It is you, the parliamentary researcher, who is usually seen to have the most glamorous role. Based at the heart of the Westminster Village, with an office inside the parliamentary estate, you have access to all areas of Parliament, including the House of Commons and the numerous bars and canteens. There is a particular air of intrigue and mystique about the role of the parliamentary researcher that has been fuelled by television shows such as *The Thick Of It*, *The West Wing* and the US remake of *House of Cards*, as well as the media coverage and narrative given to real-life figures such as Alastair Campbell, Lynton Crosby and Damian McBride, which have all projected these individuals as central characters who carry high levels of power behind their boss's throne.

The Guardian's parliamentary sketch writer John Crace calls parliamentary researchers 'the most terrifying species of all' who work in Westminster:

> ...almost all of whom are under thirty, look as if they are under twenty and, if all goes well, will be MPs themselves within five years. They walk at twice the pace of everyone else and their eyes burn twice as fiercely; they have the certainty of their convictions yet none of the responsibility for the consequences. They also might that morning have drafted a clause in a bill that could make life either a bit better or bit worse for hundreds of thousands of people. It doesn't really matter too much which. What counts is that they've done it.[16]

It is true that some parliamentary researchers can, as former Liberal Democrat parliamentary researcher Oliver Campion-Awwad says, 'have an active role in influencing their boss's outlook'[17] and their work can have important impacts on people across the country. Your day-to-day role is to support the MP's duties in Parliament. This means you'll carry out the majority of research ahead of debates and speeches, provide advice on Oral and Written Questions and assist with any portfolio role your boss may have, such as a shadow ministerial position or being a member of a select committee. You will, quite literally, put words in your MP's mouth. You will have your ideas for questions or Facebook posts acted upon and speeches you've written read out in the House of Commons. One former parliamentary researcher recalls, 'I was so excited and proud the first time I heard my boss read out in the Commons a speech I had written for her. I grabbed as many copies of Hansard as I could and posted them to all my family.'

---

16 'The Insider's Guide to Westminster: From Portcullis House to the Burma Road', John Crace, *The Guardian*, 14 May 2015

17 'An MPs Office: Who Are These People...?', Oliver Campion-Awwad, *Public Affairs Jobs HQ*, http://publicaffairsjobshq.com/an-mps-office-who-are-these-people

It's likely you will lead on the MP's media relations. Your closeness to the action in the Commons means you should be quick at spotting opportunities for your boss to make interventions that can, in turn, be used as a press release or, more recently, for tweets, Facebook posts and infographics. Your physical proximity to the broadcast media matters too. Just a two-minute walk south from the House of Commons is 4 Millbank, home to the BBC, ITN and Sky News Westminster radio and TV studios. As Emma Hutchinson, *ITV News*'s regional political correspondent, explains later, you will organise the majority of an MP's broadcast appearances through the reporters and producers based at these studios. The route between Parliament and 4 Millbank bustles with MPs and staffers shuttling back and forth to provide comment and reaction to the main news of the day.

In today's era of soundbites and key messages, you need particular skills to help your boss perform in front of a microphone. As this book will show, first, you need to be on good terms with the reporters, producers and cameramen who cover your MP's broadcast region. The key to this is understanding their deadlines and the pressures that the media work under. Similarly, if you or your MP are unhelpful and consistently turns up late for interviews, then the reporter will always opt for someone who is more cooperative. Second, you need to know the party's 'top lines' on the issue to be discussed in the interview, or, if you don't, you need to know how to find them fast, and often while on the move (for example, make sure you have stored the mobile numbers of the people who work in the party's media team at HQ). Third, you need to learn to role-play the interviewer. Many MPs will want to practise before going live, so take some time beforehand to predict the questions, challenge your boss's responses and offer advice and ideas to improve their answers.

Your research, writing and communication skills, along with your judgement, ability to think quickly and work across many different tasks over long hours will have a significant impact on the performance of your boss. The more in control and on top of things you are, the more your MP can focus on their performance during parliamentary debates, on the radio or on TV, or in the various meetings and engagements they attend each day in Westminster.

Being so integral to an MP's parliamentary duties means that, over time, a parliamentary researcher can grow to become a very influential person in the Westminster Village. You will not only learn the ins and outs of how Parliament works, but you'll get to know many people and lots of insider information. Some consider the job to be the perfect apprenticeship for becoming an MP. Whether it is this insider knowledge of how the parliamentary system works, the network of people you come to know or your proximity to the centre of power (or more likely a combination of all three of these factors), there is certainly something about the role of parliamentary researcher that ignites a latent desire in many to run for office themselves. (You should therefore expect most people you meet at social events to ask if you aspire to be an MP one day.)

At the beginning of 2015, 30 per cent of the Cabinet had previously worked for an MP in some capacity earlier in their careers. That so many staffers rise to become MPs, ministers, secretaries of state – and in the case of David Cameron, Prime Minister – has further added to the sense of influence and intrigue surrounding your role as a parliamentary researcher. However, to some, this opportunity for staffers to quickly move up through the political ranks merely projects a system that is rife with cronyism, insiderism and nepotism.

This is not just a UK trend, but a worldwide one. As the professionalisation of politics has spread, it has coined the term 'career politician'. In 2013, former UK Prime Minister Tony Blair, who was a lawyer before becoming an MP, said he believed there was a 'general problem' in Western democracies with career politicians who have never worked outside the political sphere. Speaking to *The Independent*, Mr Blair said:

> I advise any young person who wants to go into politics today: go and spend some time out of politics. Go and work for a community organisation, a business, start your own business; do anything that isn't politics for at least several years. And then, when you come back into politics, you will find you are so much better able to see the world and how it functions properly ... this is an issue that they're debating in the US right now, in many places in Europe, and I do think there is a big gene pool problem with modern politics.[18]

Not all parliamentary researchers go on to become MPs, however, and you will find many aspects of your role to be far from glamorous – it's not all about set-piece speeches and schmoozing with Laura Kuenssberg. A significant and growing proportion of your time is likely to be taken up by jobs that many staffers bemoan, such as writing letters to constituents regarding policy matters, arranging visits, or giving tours around the parliamentary estate. Unfortunately for some unlucky parliamentary researchers, their time is occupied by running personal errands for the MP, avoiding temper tantrums or covering up for their boss while they escape on a secret holiday. Though these jobs are indeed less exciting politically, and are certainly not the roles depicted in the television programmes or recalled in the memoirs of former aides, you should consider them to be just as important as the other duties you carry out. Why? Because these acts serve to directly connect and engage the voter with their elected representative and with the parliamentary process; exactly the sort of interaction required if MPs are ever going to rebuild a trusted relationship with the general public.

18 'How I became Prime Minister of the world', Tony Blair, *The Independent*, 28 October 2013

Over the course of a year, an MP can expect to receive well over 10,000 emails, letters and tweets from constituents, many of which will be lobbying them on a particular policy issue. As with casework, the issues that concern constituents vary immensely: anything from immigration to international development; from funding for cancer research to alcohol and fuel duties. New parliamentary researchers are often surprised to discover that animal welfare tends to get constituents contacting their MP the most. 'Over the last couple of years thousands of people have lobbied my boss over the badger culls, fox hunting, the use of wild animals in circuses, the breeding and selling of puppies and the health of the global bee population,' says one staffer, 'and my boss is a London MP with very little wildlife or green space in his area.' To demonstrate the British public's desire to speak up on behalf of animals, we can look at the RSPCA's 'Vote for Bob' project. This initiative called for greater political protection for the UK's natural environment and wildlife. Prior to the 2015 general election, it gained the support of over 120,000 people who either emailed or tweeted their local candidates to ask them to do likewise. By the time of polling day, 1,089 prospective parliamentary candidates (PPCs) had publicly backed the Vote for Bob campaign, largely as a result of this lobbying from local people.

Mass email and social media campaigns like 'Vote for Bob' have been made possible by digital technology breaking down the traditional barriers to participating in the act of lobbying an MP. The term 'lobbying', an activity that seeks to influence decisions made by a government and/or lawmakers, originates from the corridors and hallways (i.e. the 'lobbies') around the House of Commons. It used to be the case that if a member of the public wanted to meet their MP and seek their representation on a particular issue then he or she would have to travel down to Parliament and discuss the matter with the MP in one of the lobbies.

Nowadays, most voters do it by email, Facebook or Twitter. As Matthew Pennycook discovered shortly after being elected, posting on Twitter: 'My parliamentary inbox rapidly filling up with emails from concerned constituents opposed to fox hunting, badger culls and seal slaughter.'[19] Simple digital technology is able to link a person's postcode to their local MP's email and social media. This now means that charities and pressure groups such as RSPCA and 38 Degrees can quickly and effectively rally their members to 'Email or Tweet your MP' to ask them to support a particular issue or cause, back an amendment to a Bill, sign an EDM or attend a briefing event in Parliament that they're organising.

If an MP is to build a positive reputation among their local electorate then, just as it is important to take on all the casework they can, it is vital that you ensure they respond to each and every piece of correspondence. If a constituent has taken the time to email their MP, even if they have done little more than click the 'Email your MP' button (in the majority of cases the main text for the email will have been pre-set by the charity or pressure group), it is right that they should expect to receive a response and feel that their views have been listened to and taken on board. The outcome of this for parliamentary researchers is that most working days will end with you being required to spend thirty minutes folding letters and stuffing envelopes.

As with casework, the vast majority of MPs and their staff accept this growing aspect of their role and do try to respond as fully and quickly as possible. There are some MPs, however, who expostulate when a particular campaign stirs a lot of constituents to get in touch with them. In 2010, the newly elected Dominic Raab, MP for Esher and Walton, wrote to 38 Degrees about their practice, complaining: 'There are hundreds of campaign groups like yours, and flooding MPs inboxes with pro-forma emails creates an undue

---

19 www.twitter.com/mtpennycook, 22 May 2015

administrative burden.'[20] The website rejected Mr Raab's repeated requests to be taken off their mailing system and later published the entire email thread with Mr Raab, which demonstrates that you should always be aware that any email you send could be leaked or screen-grabbed, posted online and used against your boss.[21]

Many MPs will privately agree that these online lobbying campaign tactics have created additional work, which can at times become overwhelming, particularly when there is a contentious vote in the Commons, such as on same-sex marriage, fracking or the Transatlantic Trade and Investment Partnership (TTIP), going on. At these times, in just one week the MP could receive well over 1,000 emails, tweets or messages over Facebook. When the government announced it was to hold a vote on relaxing the Fox Hunting Act in July 2015, one researcher describes his boss's inbox as 'going nuts', with a flood of constituents arguing either for or against the reforms. Whatever the issue though, most MPs believe that the duty of being a responsive and responsible democratically elected representative by far outweighs the occasional inconvenience of having their inbox filled with hundreds of copies of the same, pro-forma email.

In fact, MPs and parliamentary researchers are starting to realise that these campaigns can be used to their advantage, in that they are a gateway to building a more engaged relationship with a constituent. First, the exchanges help to promote positive relationships between an MP and their electorate. Nowadays, very little good news arrives in the post, so to receive a letter from your

---

20 See blog.38degrees.org.uk/2010/08/09/dominic-raab-tells-constituents-dont-email-me/

21 Another good example of this is the publication of a letter sent by Tobias Ellwood MP to IPSA in support of a pay rise for MPs. Mr Ellwood, who also earns a ministerial salary, complained in the letter: 'I never expected to be watching the pennies at my age and yet this is what I now have to do.' A copy of this letter was published by *The Independent* and lead to a torrent of criticism from the public. Twenty-four hours later, Mr Ellwood issued an apology on his Facebook page that said: 'I recognise that this was inappropriate and insensitive. Constituents' comments have been a stark personal reminder of the challenges everyone is facing and I am the wiser for it. I apologise for the offence I've caused.'

local MP, in a nice Houses of Parliament envelope and written on embossed paper, is for most people a pleasant and welcome surprise. Many MPs will often feed back to their parliamentary researcher positive comments they've heard on the doorsteps from residents who have received a letter from them. One member, who represents a marginal seat, explained that: 'Quite a few times constituents have told me they've stuck my letter on their fridge door or placed one on top of the fireplace. They tell me they show it to all their friends and family when they visit. You can't beat publicity like that.'

As well as building better relationships with constituents by responding to this correspondence, MPs have a huge opportunity to seize the initiative and communicate proactively and consistently with thousands of their constituents at minimal cost. Data-gathering has over recent years become a major buzzword in politics, as it has in online marketing in general, with all political parties testing different sorts of sign-ups, surveys and share buttons across their websites and social media channels to help them build vast databases of voter contact details and their political persuasions.

In your own, smaller way, you should look to use the information that constituents provide in these policy-lobbying emails as part of your own data-gathering strategy. All constituents who email in could, for example, be added to your MP's e-newsletter mailing list. This weekly or monthly update will inform constituents about the MP's recent activities locally and in Parliament. Mass email technology such as Mailchimp and NationBuilder offer reasonably cheap platforms for this. Done well, these e-newsletters can prove to be very effective for an MP, bolstering their support and increasing name recognition and familiarity among their constituents. At the very least, just the act of an e-newsletter landing in a constituent's inbox forces them to make a decision about whether they choose to read it, ignore it or delete it. Whichever they choose, they are still engaging with the MP on some level.

The second crucial role assistants bemoan, but which is hugely beneficial to their boss's reputation, is arranging for constituents to visit Parliament. This is done by either booking the group on one of the official 'Members' Tours' around the parliamentary estate or on the tour up Big Ben. You will also regularly give tours yourself. On a normal weekday, when the Commons is sitting, you can take up to six guests around the estate. With your official accreditation you can take the group around all the places the official tours go, as well as some additional ones that are off the tourists' beaten track. This includes the Chapel of St Mary Undercroft (a Church of England chapel just off Westminster Hall, where both Margaret Thatcher and Tony Benn laid in rest the night before their funeral services), the terrace overlooking the Thames where MPs tend to drink on warm summer evenings while they await late votes. Although officially against the rules you may also want to impress by taking them up onto the roof of the House of Commons, which boasts an incredible view of Big Ben that, when lit up, resembles a hologram emerging from the Commons chamber. Your boss may also ask you to go on the hunt for tickets to Prime Minister's Questions (of which there is an unofficial black market among staffers), where your guests will experience the real-life theatre of a House of Commons full with its 650 members.

Drafting speeches, Questions or amendments to a Bill, preparing the MP for a media interview, responding to the latest policy campaign, devising data-gathering strategies, giving tours of Parliament or finding PMQ tickets – all of this illustrates the huge variety in roles you will be expected to carry out. Since their introduction, parliamentary researchers have become indispensable for MPs and will continue to be so as the rules of engagement and political participation are re-written by digital technology.

• • •

THE CORE ROLES expected of a caseworker are to manage and progress pieces of casework that the MP has agreed to take up on behalf of a constituent. The issues vary, with child support, asylum and immigration, housing problems, benefits, neighbour disputes, problems with local NHS services and employment issues being just some that feature regularly. Lynsey Tod, who worked as a caseworker at separate times for Andy Sawford and Nick Raynsford, says:

> When you work in the constituency office, you are working at the coalface. You are dealing directly with the people who elected your boss to be their representative and your duty is to them as much as it is to the Member of Parliament you work for. The issues that come across your desk on a daily basis are as varied as you could possibly imagine. From the wave of dustbin lid thefts (I kid you not) to the imprisonment of a constituent overseas, or the constituent who has run out of food bank vouchers because their benefits have been sanctioned, to the muddy footpath which has been preventing elderly residents from accessing their nearest bus stop. Often constituents turn to their MP as a last resort, when they have tried everything they can think of. It requires patience, but more importantly, you need to be respectful and understand that however you may personally view their issue, it is the most important problem the constituent is experiencing in their life at that moment. You are their voice and it's your job to make sure they are heard. You don't always win but if you can show that you have respected their views, have shown that you empathise with their predicament and have made an effort to assist, you would be surprised at the respect you and the MP get back in return. Ultimately, through casework you have the power and opportunity to make a positive difference in someone's life and at the end of the day that's what politics is all about.

Casework begins with a constituent contacting their MP to ask for help. Traditionally, this begins with a face-to-face meeting at one of the MP's help and advice surgeries (which the caseworker will attend too), however, many constituents now find it easier to call, email or even make initial contact through social media. The caseworker is then responsible for taking follow-up actions on behalf of the constituent, such as by writing letters to local and national government departments or putting in calls to a relevant agency or organisation.

Not all cases are resolved quickly or easily, and the caseworker will advise the MP on next steps to escalate the matter. MPs will often use the House of Commons to raise an issue directly with the relevant secretary of state or minister, asking them to personally intervene or meet with the MP and the constituent to talk through the case. If this still fails, an MP may seek to raise the case with the Prime Minister during Prime Minister's Questions (this will have the added benefit of securing local press coverage). The MP will also look to their caseworker to keep them informed about the frontline impact of government policies, such as changes in social security and the relationship between the use of payday lenders and local foodbanks, as these may be issues that could be campaigned on at a local or national level. Lynsey Tod explains that:

> What happens in the constituency office is usually a microcosm of what is happening across the country and it can help MPs to identify where attention is needed the most. It was the casework issues that arose in Andy Sawford's by-election that resulted in the tabling of Private Members' Bills to tackle zero-hours contracts and to regulate the behaviour of some employment agencies. It was the cases that MPs were dealing with across the country that encouraged the Public Accounts Committee and the DWP [Department for Work and Pensions] Select Committees to investigate companies like Atos

> and Capita, who held the contracts for the Work Capability Assessment and PIP [Personal Independence Payment] assessments.

Casework tends to be complex and can take a long time to resolve, so MPs need their caseworker to be dogged, thorough, patient and possess excellent organisational skills to monitor and log all correspondence. Over time, a caseworker is likely to become somewhat of an expert in particular policy areas. Naturally, this will tend to reflect the local characteristics of the constituency their MP represents; if, for example, the constituency has a particular issue with local housing stock then the caseworker will become highly skilled in all matters concerning repairs, rental agreements and housing benefits, as well as dealing with housing associations, developers and local government authorities.

The role of a caseworker is incredibly important; their primary duty is to help resolve issues in a person's life at often particularly difficult or harrowing times. While there is some training available for new caseworkers, sometimes this comes too late. One caseworkers states:

> About a week after I started, I had a constituent in tears wanting me to sort out their mother's asylum case. A few hours later I got an email from the same person, stating that she couldn't handle all the stress of dealing with the Home Office and that she was going to commit suicide. I frantically rang around other MPs' offices asking for advice. In the end I managed to get an on-call psychotherapist round to the constituent's house to calm her down, assess her mental health and ensure she wouldn't do what she said she would in the email.

Caseworkers are extremely effective. They will, on average, deal with over 1,000 constituents a year and will successfully resolve most of their cases. For some constituents, the help they receive from a caseworker leads to life-changing results, from securing a person's right to remain with their family in the UK, to finding them a new, safe and warm home. It is unsurprising that, scattering the walls and cabinets around a caseworker's desk, there will often be a collection of thank-you cards, letters and small tokens of gratitude for their efforts.

• • •

IF THE ROLES of the parliamentary researcher and the caseworker are to assist the MP with his or her public-facing performances, it is mostly the job of the office manager and the secretary to make sure that all the internal operations are in order and running smoothly. The office manager will have overall responsibility of these duties and will usually be the most senior of all the staffers.

In today's hostile climate towards MPs, by far the most important job for an office manager is to ensure that the expenses are in order and no journalist has reason to make a story out of them. Since the new expenses system was set up by IPSA, MPs have lamented its complexity and the amount of time it takes to input information. After trying to figure it out first for themselves, many MPs quickly determine to devolve responsibility to their office manager.

MPs' expenses remain confusing and the headline figure that a certain MP has claimed 'X amount in a year' is often misleading. This is not necessarily the fault of the journalist reporting the data; the problem lies in the way the data is first published. Under the headline figure, an MP's expenses are divided into many different sections, such as their staffing budget (which accounts for over three-quarters of the total amount), accommodation, constituency office rent, office stationery (MPs spend thousands each year on paper, ink and postage), and travel – these categories should be more clearly identified when expenses data is released.

It is usually the office manager who keeps track of all the separate budgets and makes sure the MP is not overspending and is filing claims correctly.

The office manager can also be thought of as playing the role of a filter, and the clearest example of this will be their management of the MP's primary email address. One shrewd innovation by the parliamentary ICT department, known as 'PICT', has been to provide MPs with two email addresses – one for all public-facing work, such as for use on the MP's personal website, parliament.uk, TheyWorkForYou and lobbying or casework from constituents, and another email address for internal emails with their staff or other MPs. This second email address should not be interpreted as an attempt by MPs to shield themselves from their constituents; owing to the high volume of emails they receive, MPs need this degree of separation otherwise they will never be able to identify the emails they need to act upon immediately from those that they can trust their staff to deal with.

In many offices, it will be the task of the office manager to look after the public-facing account and forward emails on to the relevant staffer to handle. Matters concerning Parliament or policy campaigns will go to the parliamentary researcher, diary issues to the secretary, all casework goes to the caseworker and any other issues will either be dealt with directly by the office manager or if necessary raised with the MP.

The office manager will endeavour to refer as few issues as possible to the MP – preferring to give them the time and space to focus on the other activities and commitments in the diary that day. As such, they will act on behalf of the MP across a wide range of local issues. It is essential, therefore, for them to have good diplomatic skills (especially for dealing with internal local party issues). An MP does not have the time to deal with every slight dispute or disturbance that may bubble up in the constituency while they are away in Westminster, so they will value an office manager who is able to step in, dilute and resolve issues on their behalf.

When an MP is away in Parliament, their office manager will also represent them in any formal meetings that take place across the constituency. These could be police, health committee or council meetings, or perhaps a community gathering to discuss a local issue, such as plans to build a new factory or windfarm somewhere nearby. In these meetings, the office manager will often be expected to emphasise the efforts the MP is already making to assist the residents in their cause, while at the same time taking away ideas for further intervention. During the course of attending meetings and dealing with problems, the office manager will seek to keep well informed of current opinions and to pick up on any information, rumour or gossip that it would be prudent for their boss to know.

• • •

THE FINAL PIECE of the jigsaw making up an MP's office is completed by the secretary, whose key responsibility is managing the MP's diary. Due to the growing demands on today's MPs, time has become an ever scarcer and precious resource, and it takes a good secretary to make sure the diary runs smoothly.

First, there is a framework the diary must fit around. The most important part of this is the whip (traditionally a piece of paper but now also communicated digitally) that is circulated every week by each party's Chief Whip. The whip sets out upcoming votes and when MPs are expected to be in Parliament. If the vote is underlined three times on the whip (making it a 'three-line whip'), then other than for exceptional reasons, the MP is required to vote, and do so in the way that toes the party line. If, on the other hand, the vote is only underlined once (a 'single-line whip'), the MP is allowed to remain in the constituency to focus on local issues without seeking prior permission to be absent from the Chief Whip. As MPs become ever more constituency-focused, the House of Commons often sits close to empty on days when there is a single-line whip in place for the major political parties.

Second, the diary must fit in with the MP's schedule of help and advice surgeries across the constituency and canvassing (otherwise known as 'door-knocking') sessions.

Surgeries tend to take place on a Friday or Saturday morning, with canvassing taking place on a Saturday afternoon – or in the morning if there isn't a surgery. Increasingly, MPs, especially those in marginal seats, are looking to squeeze in extra canvassing sessions on a Monday morning or a Thursday afternoon – days when there is most likely to be a single-line whip.

Within this framework, the secretary will liaise with other staffers to set up visits, meetings and activities for the MP across the constituency and in Westminster. They will ensure relevant information is attached inside their online diary, such as background research compiled by the parliamentary researcher or caseworker as well as names of attendees and the location of the visit.

Finally, the secretary must be respectful of the MP's desire to fit in time with their family, especially if he or she has young children. Changes to the sitting times of the Commons have helped MPs to see more of their family. The Commons used to sit at 2.30 p.m. and usually rise twelve hours later, but in 2012 this was changed to earlier starts and finishes (the House now rises at 7.30 p.m. on Tuesdays and Wednesdays and 5.30 p.m. on Thursday). Despite this, two-thirds of MPs have a family that live outside London, meaning they must still leave them on a Monday and not return until Thursday. Understandably, those with young children like to ensure they don't have too many early Monday or Friday morning meetings so they can do the school run on these days.

• • •

THE ROLE OF the MP is forever evolving, which means so too must the roles their staff perform. Forces of change are coming from the top down, in terms of the recommendations made in the *Speaker's Commission on Digital Democracy*, changes in sitting times, the opening of a nursery to make the Commons more family friendly and the IPSA-led publication of expenses data. Forces of change are also coming from the bottom up. Change.org, 38 Degrees and pressure groups like the RSPCA are creating platforms for people to take political actions online. TheyWorkForYou has made it easier than ever before for constituents to track and monitor their MP's every activity in Parliament. In response, some MPs are looking to innovate themselves. Caroline Lucas MP, for example, has published on her website the details of the meetings she has held or attended since she was elected in 2010; lots of MPs now set up special Q&A sessions on Facebook or Twitter, while others are organising coach trips that bring constituents down to see Parliament for themselves. The MP might get the credit for these initiatives, but it is you who will have made them happen.

IPSA'S JOB DESCRIPTIONS:[22]

Parliamentary assistant:

KEY RESPONSIBILITIES	SENIOR RESPONSIBILITIES
Undertake research, usually from readily available sources, on straightforward subjects	Undertake research on complex and/or difficult subjects
Analyse, evaluate and interpret data to ensure the MP is accurately informed on key issues	Analyse, evaluate and interpret data to ensure the member is accurately informed on key issues
Develop and maintain current knowledge of bills, Early Day Motions, legislation, Hansard, debates, etc.	Prepare and present results for the purposes of briefing notes for committees, Parliamentary Questions, articles and press releases
Monitor media coverage and brief the MP on relevant issues	Respond to routine correspondence and enquiries from constituents, the media, lobbyists and pressure groups
Ensure the MP is fully briefed on potential Questions and motions to be put to the House	Monitor media coverage and brief the MP accordingly
Give advice on policy issues	Advise the MP on policy issues
Supervise staff members where appropriate	Ownership of diary management
Project work	Progress casework as required
Progress casework as required	Research local, regional or national issues to support the MP's work
	Deal with complex queries and complaints on MP's behalf, including drafting and signing letters
	Undertake supervisory responsibility as required
	Lead on project work as required

22 See http://parliamentarystandards.org.uk/Job%20Description/Documents/MP%20staff%20JDs%20spreadsheet%2015%20-%2016.pdf

Caseworker:

Key responsibilities	Senior responsibilities
Attending surgeries and other meetings as appropriate	Attend surgeries, tribunals and meetings as appropriate
Dealing with standard queries from members of the public	Liaise with government agencies, voluntary sector and others to resolve constituency matters
Gathering relevant information to assist with resolving cases	Take initial action on queries from members of the public, including responding on behalf of the MP as appropriate
Log all cases; monitor progress and ensure all identified actions are taken	Gather relevant information to resolve or progress cases
Retain records and information confidentially and in line with the Data Protection Act	Develop knowledge in specialist areas
Draft responses to constituents	Ensure all cases are logged; monitor progress and ensure all identified actions are taken
Analyse patterns of enquiries and produce reports	Ensure records are kept and information managed confidentially and in line with the Data Protection Act
	Provide briefings for the MP
	Monitor media coverage, liaise with media, prepare press releases as required (on constituency, non-party political matters)
	Supervise other members of staff
	Respond to routine correspondence and enquiries from constituents, the media, lobbyists and pressure groups
	Manage and progress portfolio of casework appropriately
	Research local, regional or national issues to support the MP's work
	Manage projects
	Analyse, evaluate and interpret data to ensure the MP is accurately informed on key issues and is aware of trends

Office manager:

Key responsibilities
Responsibility for managing all aspects of the budget, keeping the member informed of all relevant financial matters
Ensure a range of efficient secretarial and administrative support
Manage the office team, ensuring accurate personnel records are kept and notifying IPSA of contractual changes as necessary
Manage secretarial support to special interest groups as required
Ensure the office is fully equipped
Overall management of the member's diary commitments, delegating tasks to others as appropriate
Liaise with groups/personnel at Westminster, within the constituency and the general public on the member's behalf as necessary

Secretary/Personal assistant:

Key responsibilities	Senior responsibilities
Opening and despatching mail	Manage and monitor incoming calls and enquiries
Diary management	Efficient data and file management to comply with Data Protection Act
Assisting with arrangements for events (non-political)	Deal with complex queries and complaints on the MP's behalf, including drafting and signing letters
Responding to enquiries by telephone and email, passing on queries to other team members/MP as appropriate	Manage the MP's diary commitments with overall control of constituency commitments
Providing administrative support in relation to MP's expenses scheme	Ensure enquiries are dealt with sensitively and confidentially
Handling administrative arrangements for meetings with members of the public/MP surgeries	Maintain up-to-date knowledge of relevant legislation
Photocopying, filing, record-keeping and typing correspondence	Supervise staff as required
Liaise with external suppliers when required regarding office supplies	Manage budgets as required
	Provide secretarial support to special interest groups as required
	Supervise other members of staff

Chapter 3

How to get a job as a parliamentary researcher

TO MEMBERS OF the public, Parliament can look like a difficult place to get into. The estate is surrounded by high, heavy-duty iron railings and, at each entrance, special forces police officers stand clutching machine guns while keeping a watchful eye over people going through the airport-style bag and body scanners. Once inside, all visitors must wear a paper pass to say that they have been through the security checks and their movements are limited to just a few areas of the parliamentary estate – Westminster Hall, Central Lobby and the committee room corridor.

Similarly, if you one day aspire to work in an MP's parliamentary office you may feel the task of securing a job to be equally daunting. Competition for places is fierce and there can be many barriers to entry. Despite there being around 3,000 jobs available in all MPs offices combined, each position is likely to receive hundreds of applications – especially for the parliamentary researcher roles.

There are several factors that draw so many people to want to work for an MP. For parliamentary researchers, the first factor may be intrigue; the ability to learn how Parliament works first hand, experience its traditions and quirks and work to the rhythm of Big Ben's chimes. Parliament has its own language, its own customs and is a truly unique setting in which to earn a salary.

Another pull is the lure of being close to power – and the powerful. The Houses of Parliament are of course the place where some of the most important events in Britain's political history have taken place, from the trial of Charles I to the creation of legislation that introduced the National Health Service. Westminster Hall remains to politics what Wembley Stadium is to world football: it is a place where many aspire to perform, but very few ever get the opportunity. Only the likes of Nelson Mandela, Barack Obama and Aung San Suu Kyi have over recent years been granted the honour of addressing members of both the House of Commons and Lords in the great hall. Big Ben remains the most impressive clock tower ever built and is a hugely popular tourist attraction, which people fly thousands of miles to see. Finally, democracies from all over the world look to Westminster for inspiration and guidance for how to run their legislature. As well as working daily at the centre of all of this, you are likely to find yourself regularly walking by the Prime Minister in the atrium of Portcullis House, standing in the lift with a former Chancellor or drinking in the bars next to a celebrity or famous journalist. If your boss is a minister you may often be required to collect or deliver their red briefcase.

Other people are drawn to becoming a parliamentary researcher by a particular policy area or cause and see a role with an MP as the best opportunity to push for change, promote their ideas and act on their beliefs. A former parliamentary researcher, whose MP was at the time a leading voice in their party's work on energy and climate change policy, said:

> I'm really interested in international environmental issues – it's what I studied at university and I was involved in various campaigns while I was a student. My first job out of university was for a think tank – but I quickly grew frustrated by the lack of frontline work I was able to get involved in and the slow pace of our organisation's work. By working for an MP involved in environmental policy I had much more opportunity to act on my interests, learn the latest in science (through the experts from across the world who would come to meet my boss in Parliament) and play a role in setting my party's agenda. It was a hugely fulfilling role.

Similar motivations tend to apply to the staffers who work in the constituency-based roles of office manager and caseworker, although for them the closeness to power is exchanged for a desire to be involved in local activities and community issues, as well as a natural desire to help people through the MP's casework. As former caseworker Lynsey Tod says in Chapter 2: 'Through casework you have the power and opportunity to make a positive difference in someone's life and at the end of the day that's what politics is all about.'

As well as all these elements that make working for an MP a desirable, interesting and fulfilling job in the present, many staffers see the role as a great platform from which to secure more lucrative employment in the future. Succeeding as a parliamentary researcher demonstrates you to be responsible, trustworthy and possess an ability to secure results under pressure. Having an MP as a reference adds a lot of credibility to a CV and LinkedIn profile. Through campaigns, meetings and social events, you will build the connections, networks and CV-boosting experiences in parliamentary procedure, public affairs and media relations that can be hugely advantageous when looking for a new job elsewhere. When the time is right to move on, many parliamentary researchers go to work on the other side of the fence in lobbying, public affairs, PR, think tanks or communications.

HOW TO GET THE EXPERIENCE

Most MPs will require applicants for a position in their parliamentary office to have a degree, though what subject you studied at university is not a deciding factor over whether or not you get the job. This is for three reasons. The first is that no matter what you're taught at university about politics and political theory, political science, political history or political communications, it can't re-create the reality of life inside an MP's office, hitting fast-paced deadlines and dealing with other MPs, staffers, constituents, journalists and the wide range of organisations who seek to influence Parliament.

The second reason the subject studied at university doesn't matter so much is that most MPs favour personal characteristics of trustworthiness, responsibility and discretion over academic knowledge of the parliamentary process. As one MP says:

> The House of Commons officers are the experts in how Parliament works, so I don't need my staff to know all the ins and out of this place. I need staff who, more than anything, I can trust that no matter what the task is that needs doing, they'll get their head down and get the work finished in time.

The third element that MPs look for in applicants is past experience in politics. As the website w4mp.org says:

> The key issue is whether you have ever worked, in a voluntary or paid capacity, for an MP. The most successful applicants will have a few months of work experience for an MP. This may be in the form of voluntary work in the constituency office, for the local party, helping out during an election campaign by knocking on doors or delivering leaflets, or spending some time in the parliamentary office.[23]

MPs simply do not have the time to train a new member of staff in the same manner that a regular business would. Many – especially if they tend to have a fairly high turnover of staff – prefer to employ new staffers who have already gleaned some insight and experience inside another MP's office or through being involved in a political campaign.

The knock-on effect of this requirement for previous experience has been a surge in the number of young people working in Parliament and constituency offices on unpaid internships and placements. There are estimated to be 450 interns in Parliament at any one time, putting in up to a combined 18,000 hours of work each week. Some will be there for just a couple of weeks, or just the occasional day to see what goes on and to shadow the MP. However, many will be there – unpaid – for the best part of a parliamentary year.

Hull University, Leeds University and the London School of Economics guarantee students on their four-year politics courses that they will undertake a nine-month placement inside an MP's parliamentary office. Hull University advertise this placement on their website as 'an invaluable stepping stone to your future career in politics' and have 'a pool of more than fifty MPs across the political spectrum' into which their students will be placed.[24] Other universities run similar, but shorter, schemes. Students from

---

23 See www.w4mp.org/html/library/guides/0402_looking4job.htm

24 See www2.hull.ac.uk/ug/courses/british-politics-legislative.aspx

Queen Mary University, for example, can do a placement with an MP for one semester, working approximately two days per week around their other university modules.

Many MPs like being involved in these university-led schemes – more than anything else it provides them with a free member of staff. Taking on a student through schemes also gives the MP greater assurance of the commitment of the student, their willingness to take the role seriously and to work the extra hours necessary to ensure that tasks are completed. That you may be there for nine months means an MP can afford to instruct their permanent staff to spend time training you up and hand you real responsibility within the office – such as drafting policy letters and speeches, assisting with diary management and updating the website. Additionally, these schemes – because they are arranged through a university – are classed as a 'work experience placement', meaning that an MP who takes on a student in this way cannot be accused by his or her political opponents of using unpaid interns.

Unpaid internships cause unease among some MPs, staffers and campaigners such as the Sutton Trust or Intern Aware for the reason that they can be exploitative and favour young people from more privileged backgrounds. According to figures from the Sutton Trust: 'Taking an unpaid internship can cost an individual more than £900 a month in London' – excluding transport costs.[25] This means that thousands of talented young people who cannot afford to work for free are unable to take part in unpaid internships and are, therefore, unable to gain the crucial foundational experience most MPs want or expect in applicants to their office.

To their credit, the Houses of Parliament authorities have noticed this problem and are attempting to act to rebalance opportunities. Parliament now has three schemes that offer opportunities to individuals who are unable to take part in a lengthy,

25 See www.bbc.co.uk/news/education-29996607

unpaid internship. 'These schemes all offer participants the chance to work both for the House Service and for a Member of Parliament and provide opportunities to increase their employability for the future,' say the House authorities. 'The united aim of the three schemes is to try to reach out to the widest possible pool of talent and attract people who may not have considered a career in Parliament.'[26]

The Speaker's Parliamentary Placement Scheme aims to directly 'tackle the culture of unpaid internships by providing a nine-month paid work experience placement designed to open up Parliament to people from disadvantaged backgrounds who are interested in politics but who would not be able to work without a wage'.[27] Crucially, participants in the scheme earn a salary of £17,500 pro rata to support them to cover the costs of accommodation and transport in London. Funding of these salaries comes from a mixture of public and private sponsors, with administration of the scheme led by the Social Mobility Foundation from its establishment in 2011 until 2015, and now by the House of Commons Diversity and Inclusion Team.

The scheme was introduced by the Speaker of the House of Commons John Bercow MP and former Secretary of State Hazel Blears, along with cross-party help from then Liberal Democrat MP Jo Swinson and Conservative Eric Ollerenshaw. Describing the Speaker's scheme when it was first launched, Ms Blears said, 'I believe passionately that people from all backgrounds and parts of the UK should be able to access valuable opportunities like internships ... It is simply unfair that someone should miss out simply because they cannot afford to work for free.'[28]

---

26 See www.parliament.uk/about/working/work-placements-and-apprenticeships

27 See www.parliament.uk/about/working/work-placements-and-apprenticeships/speakers-parliamentary-placement-scheme

28 See www.parliament.uk/about/working/work-placements-and-apprenticeships/speakers-parliamentary-placement-scheme

The Speaker's scheme is hugely popular and each year around 400 people apply for just ten places. The scheme is equally popular among MPs, with more members applying than the scheme can afford. MPs are interviewed by the scheme administrators and selected on the basis of who is likely to offer an intern the best possible experience.[29]

Starting in the autumn, the interns spend Monday to Thursday working in an MP's office assisting with the duties of the parliamentary researcher. On Fridays they are placed with one of the various departments of the House of Commons, such as the parliamentary ICT office, the equalities office (ParliAble) or the House of Commons Library. These Fridays working across the different House departments allow interns the chance to understand the wider workings of Parliament, and in some cases they can lead to permanent employment. One intern who spent her Fridays working in the serjeant-at-arms office was rewarded with a role as a doorkeeper for the Commons chamber.

The effects of the scheme can be life-changing. For Katherine Thompson, it marked 'a turning point' in her life after her placement with Luciana Berger turned into a full-time job in the office. Thompson says it gave her 'an invaluable insight into the machinations of British politics. It opened up a world which had always felt so exclusive and closed off.' Christine Longworth was placed in Tim Farron MP's office and has since been appointed as a permanent parliamentary researcher. Longworth says:

> This scheme has completely changed the direction of my life for the better. As well as securing an amazing permanent job, and being proud and fulfilled with what I do for a living for the first time ever, it has improved my own confidence, self-esteem and self-worth. I've

29 I'm proud that Andy Sawford and I were selected to take part in the Speaker's Scheme

made myself and my family proud, and I couldn't have done that without the SPPS.[30]

Many interns from the Speaker's Scheme have secured permanent employment in their MP's office, while others have gone on to further education or to work in various positions in the private sector, such as with the press team at McDonalds, the Association of British Insurers, British Security Industry Association and Westminster Council.

The Parliamentary Academy Scheme, also set up in 2011 by The Creative Society and Robert Halfon MP, is the first apprentice school in the UK Parliament. It is open to individuals between the ages of sixteen and twenty-four who are non-graduates, and 'aims to broaden access to Parliament and politics by giving young people a paid apprenticeship and a recognised qualification'. The Academy Scheme is a 52-week apprenticeship (paid at the London living wage rate) and combines 'on the job' training, working in the Westminster office of an MP, and college-based training. The apprentice works in the MP's office for three days a week, with every other Thursday spent on 'off the job' training.

Writing in *The Guardian*, Martin Bright, founder and CEO of The Creative Society, outlines why he set up the scheme:

> Whenever I heard an MP challenging UK businesses to take on apprentices, I contacted them to ask if they had considered doing so themselves. The excuses were predictable: they had already spent their staff budgets, had no desk space, had no one to manage someone so young and inexperienced. But a few brave pioneers showed they were unafraid to recruit outside their usual 'friends and relatives' networks. Senior figures threw their weight behind the

30 See www.w4mp.org/speakers-parliamentary-placement-scheme-returns

> scheme, including Matthew Hancock and Nick Boles on the government side and Ed Miliband and Sadiq Khan from Labour. There have been some astonishing success stories. Hancock's apprentice, Beth Prescott, stood as a Conservative parliamentary candidate against Yvette Cooper. Alice Hannam, an apprentice in the office of Liberal Democrat Mike Crockart, former MP for Edinburgh West, landed a job with Gordon Birtwistle, apprenticeship ambassador in the coalition government.[31]

The Parliament Academy Scheme received a boost shortly after the 2015 general election when business secretary Sajid Javid MP announced he would be taking on an apprentice in his parliamentary office.[32]

Away from politics, the House of Commons Apprenticeship Scheme offers young people from London 'the opportunity to gain practical experience working for the House of Commons Service while studying for an NVQ in Business and Administration or Catering'. The scheme gives apprentices experience of working within the House of Commons Service while earning a qualification to increase their employability for the future.

Some MPs have established their own initiatives to help young people gain that all important first experience in politics. Gavin Shuker, MP for Luton South, runs a 'Summer School', which, he says, 'is one of the best things we do as an office'.

In the words of Shuker:

> Each year we train around twenty 18–24-year-olds in campaigning, project work and about politics. In their four weeks with us they spend a day in Westminster, three on residential training, and three

31 See www.theguardian.com/society/2015/jun/16/apprenticeships-young-people-skills-todays-world-training-jobs

32 See http://parliamentaryacademy.com/parliamentary-apprentice-with-sajid-javid-mp

> weeks working with local charities in my constituency on real projects that make a contribution.
>
> We get even more out of it than the young people. It's a great way to get the whole staff team out of Westminster at the quietest time of the year and to work together on a shared project. It's also an excellent way of demonstrating the values of public service we believe in. The young people are not required to be members of any political party; but I can show you local councillors and parliamentary candidates whose political experience started with our summer school.

If you are looking to gain some work experience in politics, perhaps before going to university, get in touch with your local MP directly to enquire about any opportunities that they may be able to offer you in their Westminster or constituency office. Most MPs will try to be as supportive and accommodating as possible to your request, and will usually have a waiting list of people wanting to spend time with them to learn the ropes.[33] The placements are likely to last only a few weeks – most MPs constituency offices only have room, at best, for only one spare desk. Placements, therefore, have to be short in order to give more people the opportunity. As a result, this will probably make it difficult for you to get stuck into any long-term projects, so in the main you will likely to be asked to assist with data entry and general background research for any issues the other staffers are working on at that time. However short the placement, though, an MP will offer to you a visit to Parliament to spend a day shadowing the parliamentary researcher so that you can learn how the Westminster part of the operation works. You should also offer to participate in some local canvassing or phone-bank sessions with the MP. All of this will enable you to develop a more rounded perspective of the MP's role and

---

33 Many of the people who take part in a work experience placement in an MP's office do not go on to work in politics. Despite this, however, many find the experience an eye-opening, educational and valuable insight into the role of an MP and the issues they deal with every day

the daily demands on their staff, which will all be of benefit to your CV in the future should you apply for a permanent role as a parliamentary researcher.

HOW TO APPLY FOR A JOB OR INTERNSHIP

The first step is to visit the website www.w4mpjobs.org, a popular website (and sister site of w4mp.org) that offers MPs a free platform to advertise vacancies within their office.[34] Many public affairs agencies and charities also advertise on this site, and you can refine the search facility by role, salary, location and political party.[35]

The job description will identify what the role is and outline the key tasks and skills required of applicants (these will be largely consistent with the roles set out in Chapter 2). It may also include a specific mention of any particular expertise or experience the MP is looking for; if, for example, the MP has a shadow minister brief or is a member of a select committee, they will state a preference for applicants with previous involvement in relevant or related policy areas. Similarly, if the role is based in the constituency, the job description may reference a particular long-term local campaign, or frequent casework issue such as housing, zero-hours contracts or disability assessments they'll want new staffers to have a background understanding of.

The MP will ask for your CV and a covering letter. Given the number of applicants he or she is likely to receive for the vacancy, it is advisable to ensure that both documents are no longer than one side of a sheet of A4 paper each. The pages should be written

34 MPs are also likely to post vacancies on their website and use social media to help publicise the opportunity

35 While sympathy towards the party the MP represents is expected, it is not the case that you have to be a member of the political party they represent

clearly and concisely; for every sentence ask yourself, 'What value is this adding to my application?'

As w4mp identify, this is for two reasons:

1. Whoever is reading your application does not have a lot of time, and they want to see the information they are looking for straight away. If it is crowded out by less important information, it won't get the attention it deserves.

2. It will be an important skill in the job to pick out and present relevant information in a concise way, often condensing complex subjects into one or two pages. Your application should show that you can do this.[36]

You will be directed to submit your CV and covering letter by email to a current staffer (usually the office manager). It is very important at this stage that you do not attempt to use this email to squeeze in extra content that you were unable to fit in the covering letter – it won't be taken into account and may count against you as it demonstrates an inability to present information in a concise way. An example of all your email needs to say is as follows:

> *Dear Mr/Mrs/Ms/Miss* [SURNAME],
>
> *Please find attached a CV and covering letter to support my application for the role of* [NAME OF ROLE] *in the office of* [NAME OF MP] MP.
>
> *Kind regards,*
> [YOUR NAME]

The MP will then sit down with a member of their team, usually

36 See www.w4mpold.org.uk/html/library/guides/1109_parliamentary_cv_scheme.asp

the one that the new staffer will be replacing, and go through the applications to identify those to invite for an interview. Some MPs, particularly when they first arrive in Parliament, may have very little experience of recruiting and employing staff, so they might seek impartial advice on shortlisting CVs from the employment officers in the House of Commons human resources department. It's likely that the MP or a member of their team will do a quick search on social media of all applicants they intend to interview, so spend some time before applying going through your profiles and deleting any unsuitable photos or status updates.

It is good practice for one of the MP's current staffers to respond to each applicant and let them know whether or not they have made it through to this interview process (however, if you have not received a response within a fortnight it is likely you've not been successful). If you are unsuccessful, the office manager may offer feedback on the CV and covering letter, or can refer you to the Commons human resources department for guidance on how to improve your application.

HOW TO MAKE YOUR APPLICATION STAND OUT

In 2011, a parliamentary CV scheme set out 'to help demystify the process of getting a job in Parliament'.[37] Five out of six CVs the scheme looked at were rejected for one or more of the following reasons:

- Application is not tailored.

- Failure to present relevant information.

37 See www.w4mp.org/html/library/guides/1109_parliamentary_cv_scheme.asp

- Spelling or grammatical errors.
- Poor letter etiquette.
- Over the top language and sentences that are too long.
- Too much emphasis on own needs and career ambitions.

Each MP and their office should be thought of as being a small business with its own unique brand, targets, priorities and culture. Different MPs will, therefore, be looking for different skills from applicants. While it may be tempting to go 'fishing' and send your CV and covering letter to all the MPs who have vacancies in their office, if you make the effort to tailor your applications you are likely to achieve much better results. An MP wants to feel that you are interested in working for him or her, not just any MP who'll give you a job. In the words of Paul Flynn MP, his colleagues are 'impressed by candidates who have studied your interests and personality'.

You should invest some time going through Google, the MP's website and social media channels, their Wikipedia page and TheyWorkForYou record to identify any areas where you have an interest or experience that aligns with the MP. If the MP has indicated they are looking for someone with a specific policy expertise or work experience then your CV and covering letter should focus mostly on these areas.

Time, in relation to proximity to a general election, can also affect the priorities MPs are looking for in the staff. Many new MPs, such as those elected at the 2015 general election, favour applicants who have recent experience working within Parliament or another MP's constituency office. As an example, Peter Heaton-Jones MP's job advertisement in June 2015 for a parliamentary researcher stated a preference for applicants with 'strong working knowledge of the Westminster estate, its procedures and protocol'.[38]

As a general election draws closer, MPs – especially those defending marginal seats – may favour applicants who have shown a lot of commitment to the party, for example by being an active member in their local branch or volunteering previously for the MP. On these occasions the MP is looking for someone who is prepared to spend a lot of their spare time helping out in their re-election campaign by knocking on doors, taking part in phone banks, stuffing envelopes or drafting copy for leaflets that will be hand-delivered across the constituency.

Increasingly, with the changing technological environment in which Parliament is operating, many MPs will value an applicant who is able to demonstrate that they have strong and innovative digital communication skills, such as experience managing a website, producing an engaging e-newsletter or designing eye-catching infographics. If you have experience in these areas you should show how your initiatives have in the past increased an individual's or organisation's number of followers on Twitter, grown the number of people signed up to an e-newsletter's mailing list or achieved a high number of likes and shares on Facebook.

HOW TO STRUCTURE A CV

- Include your personal details at the top of the page. This should include your name, address, phone number and email address. You are not obliged to include your date of birth.

- Use a short personal statement – the intention of this is to provide an overview of who you are and why you want to work for the MP.

38 See www.w4mpjobs.org/JobDetails.aspx?jobid=50840

- Make the most of your most relevant employment experience – show how this relates to the jobs you'll be doing in the MP's office.

- Highlight any experience you've had with the party or volunteering in another MP's office – whatever it is, this experience demonstrates you have the commitment the MP will want from you.

- List your education and qualifications in reverse chronological order.

- Identify at least two references – save on space by writing 'available on request' rather than providing their contact details.

HOW TO STRUCTURE A COVERING LETTER

Your covering letter is only likely to be read if the MP and current staffer like the look of your CV. The covering letter should be used to demonstrate your understanding of the skills the MP is looking for and how your previous experience shows you will be successful in the role. A good covering letter must be tailored to the MP that you are applying to.

There are three basic areas you need to address in your covering letter:

1. Why do you want to work for *this* MP? You should emphasise what it is about the MP's portfolio, campaigns or policy priorities that interest you. What experience do you have of working on these issues and how will this help you in this role? If you have a connection to the constituency, for example growing up in the area or going to university there, be sure to mention this.

2. What is your connection to their political party? If you are a member of the party you will want to mention how long you have been so, and how active you are in your local area. You may want to discuss your reasons for wanting to get into politics.

3. Why do you want to work in that role? It is important to demonstrate that you understand what duties are involved. For example, you should not be talking about wanting to work in Parliament and on policy development if the role is as a caseworker. You can use this as an opportunity to promote any additional skills you may have – for example conducting in-depth research, working on legislation, generating proactive media stories or building social media engagement. This final section is your chance to demonstrate why you are better for the role than the hundreds of other applicants.

Finally, the covering letter should be addressed to the MP, using the form:

Dear [Mr/Mrs/Miss/Ms] Surname MP,

HOW TO DO WELL IN AN INTERVIEW

Beth Miller's story shows how one good interview can open up a world of opportunity in Westminster:

> When I was in my final year of university, a professor put me forward for a job as a parliamentary researcher for David Blunkett. I was so nervous at the interview – David is such a well-known figure and someone I'd read loads about but he put me at ease and his dog, Cosby, helped too! Fortunately, I got the job! David employs a new student every year in order to increase social mobility; he's keen that people who wouldn't ordinarily work in Parliament have the opportunity.

> When my year was up I applied to work for Vernon Coaker MP, the shadow Defence Secretary. I've been working for him for around two years now and it's given me a big insight into the dynamics of the Labour Party and the defence brief.

MPs normally choose three to five people to invite for an interview, which will take place either in Portcullis House in Westminster (if the role is Parliament-based) or in the constituency office (if the role is constituency-based). The MP will be joined by another member of the staff – probably the staffer who is leaving, as they'll be best placed to know what the job entails and the particular skills it requires (you may, therefore, want to appeal as much to the staffer as you do the MP). If the MP has previously sought the advice of the Houses' human resources department they may wish to have one of their employment officers present to give professional advice on the interviewees.

The interview will go through a few specific questions about the role, your previous work experience and your political views. It is vital that you thoroughly prepare the key points you want to get across in your answers, such as demonstrating an understanding of the MP's 'brand', a passion for their political party, knowledge of particular policy areas or setting out what additional value you believe you can add to the office. First impressions, personal presentation and body language matter too, so always arrive early (if the interview is in Parliament arrive at least thirty minutes early in case there is a long queue at security), be dressed smartly, smile and lean in during the interview.

As well as asking questions about themselves and their office, the MP is likely to ask questions about a current Bill, or the main news story of the day, so it's worth spending some time in advance of the interview looking through the news, listening to recent episodes of *Today in Parliament* on Radio 4 and that morning's *Today* programme (the MP may ask, 'Who was the 8.10 a.m. interviewee today?').[39] You should also follow the MP on Twitter and Facebook to see what they're posting. The MP may ask you if they have any questions; it's important to use this opportunity to reinforce your interest in the MP and their campaigns, such as by asking: 'How do you plan to use the information you collected from constituents in your recent health survey to lobby the Health Secretary here in Parliament?'

A number of parliamentary researchers worked with w4mp.org to put together a list of potential questions an MP may ask in an interview:[40]

- Why do you want this job?
- What experience/skills/qualities do you have that make you suitable for this job?
- Why do you want to work for me and not another MP?
- Why are you a supporter of my party?
- Do you want to be an MP in the future?
- Would you enjoy working on my portfolio?
- Are you happy to undertake administrative tasks?
- Do you have experience managing people, such as volunteers and interns?

39 The 8.10 a.m. interview is usually the most high-profile or important interview of the *Today* programme as that is when the most people are listening

40 See www.w4mp.org/library/guides/startingout/application-tips/getting-a-job-with-an-mp-part-2-giving-a-successful-interview

- What do you think are the current weaknesses in our party's policy?
- What do you think are the big issues important to people in my constituency?
- How do you think our party is perceived by the electorate?
- What experience do you have in providing written briefings, notes, speeches, etc.?
- What experience do you have in researching media stories and placing these with journalists?
- What makes a good news story?
- What parliamentary techniques would you use to elicit certain information from the government?
- How would you prepare me for an Adjournment debate?
- How are you at dealing with stressful situations?
- How will you deal with difficult constituents?
- How will you prioritise a heavy workload?
- What is your biggest strength/weakness?

Above all, though, for many MPs the most important quality they're looking for is how easily you will fit into the team. While Beth Miller may have been nervous at the beginning of her interview with David Blunkett, he clearly knew from her personality and enthusiasm that she would work well in his office.

HOW TO GET PAID

During the debate in 1969 to permit MPs an allowance of £500 for secretarial purposes, several members rose to call for better terms and conditions for their staff. Mr Eric Heiler, MP for Liverpool Walton at the time, said:

> If the general public wants to know who are underpaid, they are here in the House of Commons – not us, but the secretaries ... we must put our secretarial assistance on a proper basis, pay and conditions must be related to the Civil Service, and there must be proper safeguards; and this must be done as soon as possible.[41]

At the time of their introduction, and for most of the remaining century, individuals who worked for an MP had no employment rights and pay remained low (in 1983 the staffing allowance was still just £11,364). To the credit of determined campaigners, this is no longer the case. Staffing budgets have been increased and IPSA, who now oversee employment contracts, ensures MPs pay staff according to the pay scales it has provided. There is now a pension scheme available for staff (with the House paying 10 per cent of their total earnings to the pension provider), as well as safeguards in place, such as redundancy payments when an MP loses their seat at the general election.

In their job advertisements an MP will usually state that the salary will be 'in line with IPSA guidelines'. This means that your pay will be up for negotiation. It's likely your MP will first offer you a salary rate below what they can afford in their staffing budget. Don't be afraid to ask for more – it's unlikely there will be much opportunity for a big pay rises in the future, and bonuses are non-existent.

---

41 Hansard, Members (Expenses and Allowances),18 December 1969 hansard.millbanksystems.com/commons/1969/dec/18/members-expenses-and-allowances#column_1693

There is a minimum and maximum salary for each job type:[42]

NATIONAL	LONDON
Junior secretary: £15,000–£22,666	Junior secretary: £17,170–£24,727
Senior secretary: £18,000–£27,818	Senior secretary: £21,000–£30,909
Office manager: £26,000–£38,121	Office manager: £30,000–£41,212
Caseworker: £16,000–£25,758	Caseworker: £19,000–£28,849
Senior caseworker: £19,000–£28,849	Senior caseworker: £23,000–£31,939
Parliamentary assistant: £20,000–£30,909	Parliamentary assistant: £23,000–£34,000
Senior parliamentary assistant: £30,000–£40,182	Senior parliamentary assistant: £33,000–£43,272

You will get your travel expenses covered, such as rail travel to the constituency should you need to go there to attend a press conference or to help with the running of a jobs fair the MP has convened.[43] You may also want to consider asking if your mobile phone contract can be claimed back as an expense. You will make a lot of calls and use most of your 3G on work-related activities.

Your MP will hold a lot of meetings in Parliament, which means you will buy a lot of tea and coffee for people. While this is cheap (a cup of tea from the canteens costs about 70p), it adds up if you have ten meetings a week. Some MPs give you cash to cover the cost of this, while others will ask you to collect receipts and claim them back through expenses.

42 See www.parliamentarystandards.org.uk for latest staffing budget allowance and salary bands

43 An MP is allocated ninety-six individual train journeys for their staff and it is unlikely they will exceed this limit

Collect all your receipts and once a month submit these to IPSA using their special drop box in Portcullis House.

• • •

AMONG 650 SMALL businesses, some will of course be better to work for than others. However, despite being overworked, underpaid and open to abuse from their boss, most parliamentary researchers will look back with positive memories of their time working inside Parliament. It's hard work, but very rewarding. It's stressful, but exciting. It's chaotic, but out of this comes many valuable experiences, ideas and skills that form the basis for you to have a successful career within the Westminster Village.

Chapter 4

What an MP wants

'As a new MP, one of the biggest challenges is building the right team. No sooner has the election euphoria subsided than you are suddenly faced with a tidal wave of letters, emails and appointment requests from lobbyists. Eager to build an outstanding reputation, you start to sprint as fast as you can on the electronic treadmill, quickly realising that they are arriving faster than you can reply. The smarter ones (not me) realise that you are better leaving the laptop in the bag and putting two days aside to interview the huge field of applicants that hang around the Westminster bubble.'

Kevin Hollinrake, elected in 2015 as MP for Thirsk and Malton.

THE FAMOUS QUOTE from American anthropologist Margaret Mead (1901–78) to 'never doubt that a small group of thoughtful, committed citizens can change the world; indeed, it is the only thing that ever has' carries resonance inside an MP's office. Staffers have the ability to develop ideas, build strategies and take actions (on behalf of their MP) that can truly and significantly change the world of many constituents: from securing a person's right to remain in the UK, safe from the persecution they would face if they went home, to fast-tracking a person's passport application through the system during the Home Office crisis in 2014 in time for a constituent to fly out to their sibling's wedding, or simply by arranging for them to visit Parliament, meet their local MP and experience the House of Commons in real life. At the same time, however, staffers can bring disruption and chaos to an MP's operations – so much so that MPs risk losing their seats if relations with their staff break down completely.

MPs shouldn't manage their staff, ultimately it should be the staff managing the MP. MPs do not have the time to micromanage their team, nor should they want to. They need to focus on their job of performing and be able to trust their staffers to do the work in the background that keeps the whole operation moving forward.

In short, MPs want you to be loyal, adaptable and entrepreneurial.

HOW TO BUILD A STRONG RELATIONSHIP WITH YOUR MP

In October 1962, President John F. Kennedy and his younger brother Bobby, then Attorney General, were photographed deep in discussion on the West Wing colonnade. The Cuban Missile Crisis was at its height and the two, standing side by side, were attempting to put together a plan to secure a peaceful solution between the United States and Russia. While the decisions made in an MP's office are not usually a matter of world peace or nuclear destruction – though votes in the Commons over going to war in Libya and Iraq have led to much bloodshed and many MPs would have had lengthy deliberations with their staff before walking through the voting lobbies – this iconic image of the Kennedy brothers represents how an effective relationship between an MP and their parliamentary researcher should look.

An MP will need to disclose private and sensitive information, explain their life ambitions and bounce around many bad ideas before settling on the right way forward. In your role in this partnership, you should demonstrate unwavering loyalty and discretion, and have the strength to challenge your MP when you think they're wrong and pick them up when they're emotionally exhausted and physically drained.

This loyalty can only be demonstrated over time, and will require you to make sacrifices in your personal life and put any ego of your own aside. It is always the MP who must claim the credit. You are expected to be on call through weekends, bank holidays and Christmas. In particular, if your boss has a media profile you will be asked to organise interviews and quotes should any major news story break. A former staffer remembers: 'The last thing I'd check on my phone at night, and the first I'd check in the morning, would be Twitter and Facebook to see if anyone had said anything about my boss, or worse, if someone has and he then got engaged in a fiery debate with them.' If the final edit of an e-newsletter doesn't come back until late on a Friday you may need to find a quiet corner of a pub from which to send it out to constituents. Last-minute speeches will be written through the night. You will work long hours, with twelve-hour days the norm rather than the exception. Often it will be necessary to get to the office before sunrise to ensure that your MP has all the speaking notes and briefings they require for the day ahead. No matter how early you start though, it's unlikely you'll leave much before 8 p.m.

A quick look at recent British prime ministers demonstrates how much value politicians place on loyalty, and rely on their long-term staffers. Anji Hunter worked for Tony Blair before he became the Labour Party leader and went on to spend four years with him in No. 10 as 'special assistant to the Prime Minister' (the BBC, when covering Hunter's departure from Downing Street wrote 'she is known to have been fiercely loyal to Blair'). David Cameron went to the same school as Ed Llewellyn, his Chief of Staff since 2005, and Gordon Brown had Ed Miliband and Ed Balls working for him in the Treasury for many years before they were elected MPs themselves. Damian McBride, close adviser to Gordon Brown at both the Treasury and No. 10, concludes that prime ministers rely on 'small groups of smart, committed loyal people prepared to sweat every last drop of blood and sacrifice their own personal lives and ambitions to get them there'.[44] While not on the same scale, MPs too will be relying on you and just a few others to work their socks off for them every day.

HOW TO DEAL WITH A BAD BOSS

Sadly, some parliamentary researchers find their MP difficult to work for and never get to experience such a strong working relationship. In 2010, the BBC reported an employment tribunal that ruled Jim Devine 'bullied and harassed' his office manager out of her job, which included making up stories that she was 'a gambling addict being investigated for fraud'.[45] The office manager was awarded a total of £35,000 in compensation, while Mr Devine

---

44 Damian McBride, *Omnirambles* (London: Biteback Publishing, 2014), p. 54

45 See www.bbc.co.uk/news/uk-scotland-edinburgh-east-fife-11547479

was barred by Labour from standing again for office and later lost his seat at the next general election.

While the story of Jim Devine is an exceptional case, many staff have to deal with peculiarities or problems with their boss. Some MPs make their staff wait in their Westminster flat for parcel deliveries, pick up their dry cleaning and book dental appointments. Staff and volunteers for one MP were required to place stickers onto leaves as part of a stunt to support his campaign to become Chair of the Environment Audit Committee. Others are subjected to items being hurled across the office and even faced with the possibility of being sacked by Post-it note. One parliamentary researcher once had to dress his MP. Following George Galloway's defeat in the 2015 general election, *Private Eye* reported that he made his parliamentary researcher 'spend most of her time running errands – shopping for his underwear, for instance, and planning his wedding'.[46] The Guido Fawkes blog reports that former MP David Ruffley once employed sixteen different members of staff within two years and that his 'man-management skills are the stuff of parliamentary folklore, and Guido hears reports of his "obnoxious" behaviour leading to bright-eyed hopefuls leaving his office in floods of tears, some binned after only days'. Apparently, 'To have been fired by Ruffers at some point is a rite of passage.'[47]

The account of one former parliamentary researcher to a high-profile MP is that:

> The most challenging part of working for my MP was the expectation on their part that I would take full blame for any mistakes they made in front of other MPs, shadow ministers, stakeholders and constituents. If that wasn't enough, she would then proceed to openly

46 *Private Eye*, No. 1392, 15–28 May 2015

47 See www.order-order.com/2013/03/04/david-ruffley-staff-saga-you-wont-like-him-whens-angry/

> criticise my 'poor decisions' in front of people to fully absolve herself of any fault.

While another states: 'I was expected to lie to cover for my boss's behaviour, activities and secret holidays. This was highly embarrassing, especially when it was openly acknowledged that the story we were pedalling was untrue.'

The difficulty is that, while an MP may have had a successful career and have held high-ranking positions before being elected, it's likely they will have worked for an organisation that had its own human resources department which maintained fair dealings between employer and employees. Or, at the other end of the spectrum, many MPs – especially the younger ones – enter Parliament having never held a leadership role nor employed their own staff. While Parliament has a human resources department MPs can call on for advice on staffing issues and support in the recruitment process, the department doesn't offer any services for those employed by MPs.

The Unite parliamentary branch is the 'only professional staff body dedicated to supporting people who work for MPs' both in Westminster and in the constituency. Despite the union's strong links with the Labour Party, it has members from across the political spectrum. Its chair, Max Freedman, says of the current system:

> There are systemic factors that lead to some of the poor employment practices in Parliament. MPs are elected with widely varying experience, with many never having previous experience as employers and the responsibilities this entails. Despite this, they are given large budgets to hire staff without an obligation to receive any training. Those MPs who follow good employment practices will choose to get training and those that don't are unlikely to. The reality is voluntary arrangements like this just don't work and fail those most in need.

This is reinforced by Sadie Smith, a parliamentary researcher who, in an article for *Total Politics*, writes: 'The problem lies with the personal power that MPs have over their staff. Bag-carriers are employed by their boss, who is their line manager, HR department and chief executive. If we have a problem with our employer, we have nowhere to go.'[48]

The nature of the relationship between an MP and their staff, with the balance of power being so heavily with the MP, makes it difficult for staffers to do anything when faced with issues such as unfair criticism and embarrassment, when asked to run personal errands or lie to other MPs and parliamentary researchers in order to cover their boss's back. Often, the only person a parliamentary researcher can make a complaint to about their boss's behaviour is their boss. In most cases, this isn't really a possibility, which leaves staffers – when facing what in most working environments would be considered abuse – the options of either leaving their job, putting up with the situation or leaking stories to journalists.

The Guido Fawkes blog receives many tip-offs for stories through disgruntled parliamentary researchers. Harry Cole, its co-editor, says, 'Leaking is a noble pursuit. When an MP is lying, or is abusing staff, it's right that this information becomes public.' Guido has significant influence in the Westminster Village. A high proportion of its 150,000 daily page-views come from within Parliament and Whitehall, and Prime Minister David Cameron is subscribed to receive its evening emails on his mobile phone. This makes leaking to Guido an effective method of bringing stories of bad MP behaviour not just to public attention, but straight to the top of government. However, it could present danger to those at the root of a story if they're not careful in covering up their tracks. Cole says:

---

48 'The Vulnerability of Political Staff Should Worry Us', Sadie Smith, *Total Politics*, 27 February 2013

> We're very careful to ensure our sources remain anonymous. We've published a guide on Guido that sets out how to leak without getting caught, and have a dedicated email address and answerphone for people to leave messages anonymously. However, about 75 per cent of our stories that originate from parliamentary researchers begin with a chat in a pub or some other face-to-face interaction.

If Guido is an unofficial channel through which parliamentary researchers can raise concerns and examples of bad employment practice, the new anti-bullying hotline introduced in 2014 is the official route. Mr Speaker, John Bercow MP, when announcing the introduction of the hotline, stated:

> Setting up a confidential phone-line ... is a step in the right direction in modernising the culture of the House of Commons, clearly signalling that, wherever the place of work, people are entitled to be treated with dignity, courtesy and respect as they carry out their work. Parliament is an extraordinary place in which to work and the House of Commons strives to be an exemplar of good employment practice.

The 'harassment hotline', as it has been dubbed, received a lukewarm welcome by some. Former parliamentary researcher Harriet Maltby said at the time:

> The majority of problems are MPs venting their own stress and frustration on their staff. While the phone line is helpful, the root cause is MPs can't deal with the stress and there's no support for them. Until you deal with the stress factor for MPs you'll never solve the problem of them being aggressive to staff.

The Unite parliamentary branch welcome the hotline, but continue campaigning for more support for staffers. Max Freedman says:

> The branch was glad that our survey evidence helped to convince the Speaker to introduce a new telephone helpline for staff. There is very clear evidence that unhealthy working cultures can develop in small, highly pressured offices. However, Parliament still lacks a professional HR department that staff can access to give them proper employment advice. For so many who work for MPs this is their first job and so they may not know what to expect or be fully aware of their rights in the workplace.

Tales of difficult MPs are not restricted to the parliamentary estate. Instead they emanate from across Whitehall. Liam Byrne MP – infamous for the note he left on his desk in 2010 as the outgoing Chief Secretary to the Treasury that said 'I'm afraid there is no money' – had previously hit the headlines for another note he'd drafted. Titled 'Working With Liam Byrne', the document lists a number of dos and don'ts regarding how staffers should behave in his office. The *Daily Telegraph* reported that Mr Byrne wrote: 'I like a cappuccino when I come in, an espresso at 3 p.m. and soup at 12.20–1 p.m.' and 'I like the papers set out in the office before I get in.' Amusingly, a spokesman for Mr Byrne at the time told the *Telegraph* that the document had been written a couple of years previously and that 'He is a highly efficient minister but has become more flexible since then. Some days, he has his soup at 1.30 p.m.'[49]

In another Whitehall department, civil servants working for Greg Barker, Minister for Energy and Climate Change between 2010 and 2014, had to abide by rules set out on behalf of his dachshund, Otto. This apparently included the dog's cushion being warmed up in the staff microwave to ensure Otto would not get too cold in the winter. One civil servant, clearly much aggrieved by the priority given to Otto, told the *Daily Mail* that Mr Barker's

49 See www.telegraph.co.uk/news/politics/3468400/Cabinet-Minister-tells-civil-servants-when-to-bring-coffee-and-soup.html

treatment of the dog 'proved he thinks more of the dog than us'. Another staffer set up a Twitter account for @OttoBigDog, proclaiming in its biography: 'I am the Big Dog at the Department of Energy and Climate Change and the proud owner of Greg Barker.'

HOW TO SUPPORT YOUR MP THROUGHOUT A PARLIAMENTARY YEAR

The content of an MP's week and the rhythm of Parliament shifts throughout the year. The priorities and roles of a parliamentary researcher must adapt to these changes. A new calendar year will bring a focus on parliamentary business, with many government Bills going through their committee stages. There can be up to six or seven Bill committees sitting each Tuesday and Thursday from 9.30 a.m. to 5 p.m., sapping the time of around 150 backbenchers and many ministers. In the constituency, the MP will be prioritising casework and visits to schools, businesses and other organisations; the wind, rain and dark nights make door-to-door canvassing difficult at this time of year.

The Chancellor's Budget around the turn of spring marks a change in activity and the policy-lobbying campaign emails to MPs will increase from constituents who are members of organisations such as CAMRA and FairFuelUK, who will be calling for a cut or freeze in alcohol and petrol duty. Depending on how the Budget is received by the media, and the four days of debate that follow in the House of Commons, it will give momentum in the polls to either the government or the opposition parties. Off the back of the Budget, all parties will increase their media, digital and real-world campaigning activity and unveil key messages as they prepare for the local, European or national elections that will be taking place in May.

After a few weeks of gossip, rumour and possibly some

high-profile resignations following these elections, the Westminster Village will be prepared for the State Opening of Parliament. Pavements around the estate will be jet-washed clean, roads within a certain proximity to Parliament will be closed down, snipers patrol rooftops, the broadcasters erect pop-up studios on College Green and the Queen's Body Guard, the Yeomen of the Guard (the oldest British military corps still in existence), will walk the cellars underneath the Houses of Parliament in search of any hidden gunpowder left by a modern-day Guy Fawkes.

The State Opening of Parliament marks the formal start of a new parliamentary session and the Queen's Speech, written by the Prime Minister and printed onto vellum (parchment made from calfskin which takes many days for the ink to dry on), sets out the government's proposed policies and legislative agenda for the year ahead. After four or five days for the backbenchers to debate the contents of the Queen's Speech, there will be a crucial vote. If a government has a secure majority this is a formality. If it's a shaky minority or a turbulent coalition then this vote becomes a key test of whether or not the Prime Minister carries the confidence of the Commons.

If all goes well the government will look to move fast and seize the initiative. 'In the first few days of a new session the first two or three major government Bills foreshadowed in the Queen's Speech will be introduced,'[50] says Sir Robert Rogers, a former Clerk of the House of Commons. For these Bills, this is the beginning of their journey through the legislative process. The Conservative government in 2015 introduced the Scotland Bill, European Union Finance Bill and EU referendum Bill for their Second Readings within the first few sitting days of the new parliament.[51] If your

---

50 Robert Rogers and Rhodri Walters, *How Parliament Works*, p. 141

51 Confusingly, Second Reading is the first opportunity for MPs to debate a Bill. At a Bill's First Reading, only its title is read out, followed by an order for the Bill to be printed

MP is a shadow minister and backbencher involved in one of these Bills (as Grace Wright shows later in this book in her section 'How to deal with a Bill'), this will be a busy period of time. Your job will be to set up meetings with relevant individuals, organisations and charities to learn their views on the Bill, read recently published select committee or think-tank reports and commission the House of Commons Library to work up some background briefings. Other parliamentary researchers will be busy too as their MP tries to squeeze in lots of meetings and events, and plan local media stories before the Commons shuts down for the summer.

MPs will – and should – take some time during the summer recess to relax, go on holiday, spend time with their family and live in the normal world for a bit. The same applies for staffers, and you should make the most of long lunch breaks on the terrace and the freedom to get out of the office before the evening rush hour. Use the summer recess to work through a backlog of policy letters; plan future events; build the foundations for a new campaign the MP will lead in the autumn; make updates to their website design and take some time to catch-up with your media contacts. Most importantly, relax and recharge your batteries.

Most MPs make the most of the long days and warm weather to do lots of door-knocking throughout the summer. They'll also be conducting visits to businesses, charities and schools across the area, which you will want to write up as a press release and Facebook post. The media refer to the summer as 'silly season' or 'slow news season' because so many people in politics, business, the arts, sport and the media are on holiday and so the airwaves and newspapers are filled with more frivolous stories. You should see this as an opportunity. Work with the constituency staffers to ensure that the MP has at least one newsworthy event each week planned in the diary during the summer, as these will be as good as guaranteed to receive prominent coverage in the local media. Before your MP goes on holiday, prepare a couple of press releases, such as on the launching of a survey they are conducting or praising GCSE results, which can be signed off in advance and sent out when the time is right. A proactive summer media strategy is most actively demonstrated by Labour's John Woodcock, MP for Barrow, who in 2013 conducted a 'Talk-To-Your-MP' bike ride, followed by a 'Your Manifesto' in 2014, which saw him pedal across many of the towns and villages in his constituency. Mr Woodcock's bike rides received nice coverage in the local *Westmorland Gazette* and will have provided plenty of opportunities for the taking of photos and videos to share on social media.

Summer recess used to last for twelve weeks, but this was changed in the aftermath of the expenses scandal to stop the annual stories in national tabloids of MPs taking '82-day summer holidays'. The Commons now sits for the first two weeks of September – though very little is achieved in this period – before falling silent again for the party conference season.

You will find the weeks building up to party conference to be busy. Your job will be to organise the MP's diary and put background briefings together for the various engagements their involved in, while trying to sort out your own accommodation and social activities. Most parliamentary researchers attend their party's conference, and the MP will want you there to ensure they have the correct speaking notes for each fringe, as well as getting to each event and meeting on time.

After each party has had its week in the media spotlight, parliament will settle in for the long autumn sitting that takes it up to the Christmas holidays. The set-piece event of this term is the Autumn Statement, where the government will outline its current assessment of the economy and what it aims to announce in the next Budget. For the backbenchers, there will be many important votes during the autumn as the government seeks to finalise Bills and the opposition and the Lords attempt to secure last-minute changes.

It's important you adapt to these different stages of the year to meet the needs of your boss. For example, your MP may be sitting on a Bill committee that takes up all of their time on Tuesdays and Thursdays for several weeks. On these days, you may have to attend many meetings on your MP's behalf. In the spring, there may be important local council elections and you may be required to draft print materials and digital infographics for local party members to use in their campaign. On the days of the Budget and the Autumn Statement, you will want to focus on arranging as many media interviews as possible, as well as generating lots of reaction content for your MP to post on their website and social media. When Parliament is sitting, it's likely your boss will be in Westminster four days of the week, but during recess periods you will go weeks without seeing them or any other member of the team.

HOW TO SUPPORT YOUR MP DAY TO DAY, WEEK TO WEEK

Underneath the key events like the Queen's Speech, the Budget and elections, there are many constants, such as casework, policy letters and meetings, as well as parliamentary duties such as speeches and Questions, and the weekly surgeries, which will take up the majority of staffers' time and concerns on a day-to-day basis. You must be alert and adapt to the unexpected events and last-minutes changes that invariably occur. Carefully planned diary schedules often get torn up at the last minute; the whip will be altered; the MP may get drawn in the ballot to ask a PMQ or to lead an Adjournment debate; a medium-sized local business can announce they're closing down their factory, or a constituent might make contact with particularly urgent casework. If the MP is a minister, shadow minister or the chair of a select committee or All Party Parliamentary Group (APPG), they may be required to speak in the chamber or to the media in response to a significant report or national news story that's broken that morning.[52]

Due to this ever-changing nature of an MP's role, they need you to be able to keep calm under pressure and quickly think through the best options for moving forward. If the MP is drawn to lead an Adjournment debate, who are the organisations you can contact to ask for background information and briefing materials? Are there any constituents you can approach to add quotes or case studies to the speech, or is there any data collected in a recent survey led by the MP that can be used? How can the MP best promote the speech before and after its delivery through their website, social media and e-newsletter? If a local business does announce plans to close in the constituency, what's the best way of getting hold of the chief executive's phone number for your MP to call? What should the MP's reaction statements to the press, and on their social media, be?

As well as supporting your MP to respond to issues as they arise, your boss will value it when you are able to bring new ideas and initiatives to improve their performance. Could the speech for the Adjournment debate be crowd-sourced? Could you arrange for those constituents mentioned in the speech to travel to Parliament to watch from the public gallery as it is delivered? For the business that is closing, could the MP set up a special taskforce to help the workers find employment elsewhere, and, if so, who else does the MP need to work with to achieve this?

52 The biggest event that can lead to change in the schedule for an MP, and their parliamentary researcher, is the reshuffle. A parliamentary researcher of a shadow minister might have devoted hundreds of hours to learning the key policy issues of the MP's brief inside out, developing relationships with all the relevant external individuals, organisations and trade journalists, only to have their boss moved to a new brief shadowing a different department. The next day they will have to begin the whole process all over again

HOW TO LEARN THE ROLE

In his book *How to Be an MP*, Paul Flynn MP's advice to his colleagues is that the perfect parliamentary researcher should have an 'added dash of curiosity and the persistence to find solutions to seemingly intractable problems. The ability to scan vast acres of material and isolate the killer points is vital.'

No parliamentary researcher begins their first day knowing how to do the job, indeed, no MP begins their first day knowing what they're doing. It takes many months, lots of errors and the occasional *The Thick of It* comedy moment – such as leading your boss into a broom closet rather than a committee room, or getting dates mixed up in the diary resulting in the MP arriving to speak at a conference a week too early – before you will feel confident that you've got the basics of the job covered.

The House offers some introductory and training sessions for new parliamentary researchers. A few offices may produce introductory packs for new staffers, but for many, training is mostly done by word of mouth from other members of the team, or the goodwill of parliamentary researchers in neighbouring offices, as and when new issues or problems arise. It would be wise for you to walk your corridor and introduce yourself to other staffers. In most areas of Parliament, offices are grouped by political party so you are likely to be surrounded by friendly faces – though parliamentary researchers tend to be equally friendly to each other regardless of political party (just as MPs of different parties are usually amicable to each other when they're not in the Commons chamber).

Each political party will also run its own informal introductory sessions for new staffers a few times each year. These meetings are worth taking part in as the programme will include an overview of how the party's parliamentary group operates, how to access briefings and other materials produced by the special advisers for the frontbench MPs, as well as basic behavioural guidance, such as how to deal with the media or what not to tweet now that you work for a Member of Parliament.

Don't try to do everything in your first day. Learn the processes and techniques of the role step by step. At every stage, each new skill is likely to become all-consuming and you will begin to feel as though there will never be any additional time in the day into which more work must be squeezed. On top of this you will have the added difficulty of not knowing how to get around the estate or where to find most of the rooms in which you are expected to meet your MP. Gradually, though, each task will become quicker and easier to perform, the corridors more familiar and the parliamentary jargon your boss uses will seem less confusing. Soon you will find that you have more time and thinking space to commit to generating new ideas for campaigns, writing better speeches, creating content for social media, organising phone banks or generating other initiatives that add value to your MP's performance.

MPs do not personally have lots of time to train up new staffers, which can be particularly difficult for parliamentary researchers who are the MP's only member of staff in Westminster. Some parliamentary researchers are even based in separate offices at the opposite end of the estate to their boss. Russell Antram worked as a parliamentary researcher for former Glasgow South MP Tom Harris, and is now the political and campaigns manager for Seb Dance MEP. Antram explains how he and Mr Harris organised time to meet and talk through upcoming work:

> We would meet up for a coffee in PCH when he came back from the constituency and during the week to go over the diary, the latest influx of policy casework responses and to plan for the week ahead. It was good to sit down and focus solely on things that needed doing. You could get sign-off for everything that needed doing, return to your office, and get on with your work. Once a plan was made it was

> usually stuck to. I wouldn't be subject, like others staffers I know, to the ever-changing whims and inner monologue of the member.

Different MPs will require their staffers to perform certain tasks in a particular way to fit in with their style or 'brand'. For some staffers this might mean delivering coffee or soup to their boss at certain times of day but, for most, these will be things like how the MP likes their diary to be organised. They may prefer meetings to be held at certain times of day, such as before the House sits, or different types of engagements to be colour-coded in the diary. Some prefer their diary to be printed out daily, others like everything stored in their mobile phone. Many MPs are particular over the presentation of their work. Some will have big header and footer banners printed on the paper that they will expect to be used when responding to constituents. This might include a photo of the MP (which is likely to be several years out of date), contact details and perhaps a slogan, which they use across all their offline and online communications. Beth Miller, who worked for David Blunkett, says: 'Due to David's blindness certain tasks were done differently; for example, he preferred tape recordings to Braille so I'd record a summary of the newspapers on a daily tape for him.' Some MPs may be quite fussy about where certain things in the office are to be kept (although usually their desk will be the messiest of everyone's) or over what stationery they use to sign letters.[53] Some MPs have additional roles, such as being a minister, chair of an APPG (both of which are discussed later in the book) or a parliamentary private secretary (who are appointed by a secretary of state or shadow secretary of state to be his or her assistant in Parliament). In either three of these cases, you will have to devote a lot of time to helping your MP fulfil their duties.

53 Staffers should always keep one of their boss's favourite pens on their person at all times. MPs often lose their pens, and so will be immensely grateful every time a staffer is able to produce a spare

One parliamentary researcher to a parliamentar
tary (PPS), explains:

> They say the PPS is the eyes and ears of the [shadow] secretary of state among the parliamentary party. That can be as proactive or reactive as the PPS and his or her boss choose. For a parliamentary researcher working for a PPS, you will be tasked with organising briefings on important policy issues or just being open to talk about concerns parliamentary colleagues may have. You need to keep an eye on what's coming up on the Order Paper, making sure a member of the [shadow or ministerial] team can cover any debates of sixty minutes or more in the chamber or Westminster Hall debates. You will also lead the organisation of departmental Questions. This involves drafting Questions with the shadow team to hand out to the parliamentary party, checking the Questions are 'in order' with the Table Office, emailing the parliamentary party to encourage MPs to table Questions, and physically printing the handout Questions for MPs to sign in the lobbies during key votes in the days before the tabling deadline for the Question session. The more MPs from your party table Questions, the more chance you have of getting the team's issues onto the Order Paper. The person to beat? The opposite number's PPS who will be doing the same to rally his or her troops to table their handout Questions!

As you learn the role, your greatest source of support will come from other parliamentary researchers and House staff. Invest time in building a large network of people you can call or email to ask for help whenever you come across a new task that you don't know how to do. Instead of trying to learn everything about the way Parliament works, it is usually much easier, and far quicker, to learn who the experts are on different issues and give them a call. This includes drawing on the knowledge of the many officers who work in Parliament. There is, for example, no need for you to struggle with the exact wording required to table an amendment to a Bill, when the officers at the Public Bills Office are happy to do this on your behalf. So while you may be physically on your own for most of your time in the office, there is a great deal of help and support available across Parliament for you to call on.

• • •

INITIALLY, YOU WILL have been recruited on a probationary contract, which, if everything goes well, will become permanent after three months. However, while walking over Westminster Bridge with his boss on the final day of his probation period, one aspiring parliamentary researcher was told that he wasn't going to be offered a permanent contract. Another was forced to re-apply for his job three times after the MP refused to give him a permanent contract.

As the previous stories show, unfortunately some MPs are just bad employers. If you're unlucky enough to work for one of these MPs you are unlikely to ever feel secure and appreciated in your work, no matter what you do. For the others, you can try to boost your influence in the office by introducing ideas that add additional value to the performance of the MP. Do this consistently well and, over time, your boss will consider you indispensable.

These new ideas and initiatives can be referred to as 'Critical Non-Essentials' – a term coined by the World Cup-winning, former England rugby coach Sir Clive Woodwood. In MPs' offices, Critical Non-Essentials have the ability to take the MP's performance above the levels expected by their constituents and turn them into 'the best MP we've ever had'. Securing extra PMQ tickets, producing a weekly media note that controls the local news agenda, creating engaging text, graphic and video content for social media and building effective data-gathering strategies are a few examples of what could be called 'Critical Non-Essentials'.

These extra jobs, though, must only be executed in addition to all the other duties you are responsible for – delivering well-organised, well-informed tours, writing speeches quickly, drafting piercing Parliamentary Questions, responding to policy-lobbying campaigns, ordering stationery, supporting the MP at party conference and assisting with any shadow minister or select committee role your MP may have.

The next chapters of this book provide a range of guides for how a parliamentary researcher should approach all these tasks.

Chapter 5

Visits, tours and PMQs

HOW TO FIND YOUR WAY AROUND

At the 2015 general election, Mhairi Black, at the age of twenty years and twenty-three days, became the youngest Member of Parliament since 1880. In a diary for the *Herald* newspaper, she describes her first impressions upon entering Parliament:

> The thing that I have found most striking is just how lovely all the doormen (and women) are, not only in their general manner, but in the great lengths they go to in order to ensure you are OK and are where you need to be. Westminster is an absolute maze, with all the nooks and crannies you could possibly imagine, so I have been lost very many times and have subsequently become very familiar with the staff! It is

> fairly difficult not to, at least momentarily, get sucked into the grandeur of the building itself. Mosaic floors, tapestries that reach the ceiling and the odd solid gold throne dotted about throughout the array of lavishly decorated rooms. Even despite the friendliness of the staff, you cannot help but feel you are in a historic and upper-class estate due to the dress code. The building itself is a fortress from which you never need leave. It has umpteen dining rooms, bars, lounges and social areas which are equipped to deal with any desire you may have.[54]

You will find the doormen and women to be equally friendly and helpful when you are lost or struggling to find the right room. As too will be all the other people who work inside the parliamentary estate. There are about 13,000 passholders within the 'maze' of Westminster: MPs, Lords, clerks, parliamentary researchers staffers, lobby reporters, serjeants at arms, police, doorkeepers, canteen staff, postal workers, tradesmen and women and the Blue Badge tour guides. The vast majority of these – no matter how long they've worked there – will get lost from time to time.

Parliamentary researchers are usually advised to call the Central Tours Office to ask if there is space for them to tag along on an official tour around the estate. A better tour, however, would be one given by another staffer in an MP's Westminster office.

This tour should include a trip to the Vote Office (which is where parliamentary and government documents such as each day's Order Paper, or copies of the Budget, can be collected), the Table Office (where MPs and their staff can table Parliamentary Questions and EDMs) as well as the other useful places in Parliament, such as the post office, the travel offices (where train tickets can be bought and collected), the House of Commons Library, the Public Bills Office, the Admissions Order Office, the gym, the hair salon, the roof of the

54 See www.heraldscotland.com/politics/scottish-politics/mhairi-blacks-diary-of-a-novice-mp-in-which-our-heroine-goes-through-the-.126259431

Commons, the shooting range under the Lords, the various cash points, post boxes and shower rooms and, of course, the different canteens and the Sports and Social Club (aside from having a dry cleaners there is everything that an MP or staffer would need to be able to live inside Parliament). It's not only important you get to know where these places are, but also get to know the people who work in them. Just as you will often need to call another MP's office to ask for help, you will benefit from being able to draw on the expertise of the people who work in these departments.

The following guide is an outline for what you need to know in order to find your way about:

- Always wear your pass. MPs often don't wear theirs, but parliamentary researchers must do so, or the security guards will stop you, take down your details and report you to your MP.

- Learn the main route from Central Lobby to Portcullis House. This is the spine of the parliamentary estate.

- In Portcullis House, as well as offices for 200 MPs and rooms for select committees, there are corner rooms that you will book on behalf of your MP when your MP wants to host a large meeting or a small, round-table event. These rooms can hold about sixteen people. Portcullis House has a vote office, a post office with a cashpoint and the drop box for sending expenses claims to IPSA (who are not based inside Parliament), a coffee shop, a large canteen, a restaurant, a quiet area for MPs to have meetings, as well as numerous tables and chairs in the main atrium.

- Running off to the west of Portcullis House is the entrance to 1 Parliament Street. Parliament Street looks more like an upmarket hotel than an office building and is home to more MPs' offices, the House of Commons Library, Bellamy's canteen, the Parliament nursery, another vote office and a few smaller rooms that MPs can book out for meetings or roundtables (though these aren't very nice and are only used when all other rooms are booked up).

- To the north of Portcullis House, past the smoking area, are the Norman Shaw South and North buildings. These contain further offices for MPs and their parliamentary researchers. The Leader of the Opposition has a suite on the second floor of Norman Shaw South; the store room for the Curator's Office (MPs and their parliamentary researchers can go down to the store room to select artwork for their office) is in the basement. In between the two Norman Shaw buildings is a small car park and spaces for cyclists to leave their bikes. The exit point, called Derby Gate, leads onto Whitehall opposite the Foreign and Commonwealth Office and the Treasury, and is next to the Red Lion pub – a popular hangout for parliamentary researchers. Parliament can be accessed twenty-four hours a day, seven days a week through the Derby Gate entrance.

- Elsewhere from Central Lobby, walking under the mosaic of St Andrew leads to two sets of stairs. Going down takes you to the terrace cafeteria, the terrace, the Strangers' Bar and many of the smaller dining rooms that are used for events and report launches. The stairs going up lead to the Committee Room corridor. This corridor equals the length of the terrace. Some of the Committee Rooms, such as CR10 and CR14, are like miniature versions of the House of Commons chamber and are used for Bill committee meetings. The smaller rooms along the Committee Room corridor used often for APPG meetings, or by MPs meeting large groups of constituents or school children.[55] All these rooms

55 Many of these rooms in the old building are now available for members of the public to hire for special occasions such as weddings. The most expensive is the Members' Dining Room and the Portcullis House Atrium, which both cost £9,000 to hire for a day. The income from this is contributing to the maintenance and renovation of the parliamentary estate

are beautifully decorated but are very cold in the winter. Most also have recording equipment inside, and it's always worth checking that this is switched off when you first enter the room (the system switchboard is usually in the far corner of the room).

- Beneath the House of Commons is the Travel Office. You will need to visit here to book train tickets, for which you will require the details of your MP's IPSA credit card.

- Under the mosaic of St Patrick leads to St Stephen's and then Westminster Hall. There is a special entrance for passholders at the south end of the great hall, which is used mostly by MPs and parliamentary researchers when shuttling to and from College Green or the TV studios at 4 Millbank to record media interviews.

As Mhairi Black discovered, everyone is usually very friendly and happy to help someone find their way when they're lost, so never be afraid to ask.

HOW TO ARRANGE TOURS AND VISITS FOR CONSTITUENTS

In the weeks when Parliament is sitting, an MP can arrange for constituents to be booked, at no cost, on professional Blue Badge guided tours around the parliamentary estate or up the Elizabeth Tower to see Big Ben strike on the hour. Constituents love visiting Parliament and seeing for themselves the estate's architecture, as well as trying to catch a glimpse of the activities taking place inside. In 2014/15, 128,434 people saw Parliament through a Member's Tour of the parliamentary estate, while 11,069 climbed the steps up to Big Ben.

Making the necessary arrangements for these tours is a reasonably straightforward administrative task. However, due to the popularity of both tours, you need a good knowledge of how the booking system works to ensure your constituents get on a tour at the time they want.

'Members' Tours' of the Houses of Parliament

Members' Tours around the parliamentary estate set off every five minutes from Westminster Hall and take seventy-five minutes to cover all the main areas, including the Queen's Robing Room, the House of Lords, the House of Commons and St Stephen's Hall. These tours can only take place when neither the MPs nor the peers are using their chambers. Members' Tours begin at the following times:

- Monday: 9.00 a.m.–12 noon (full tour)[56]
- Tuesday and Wednesday: 9.00 a.m.–9.55 a.m. (full tour)
- Tuesday and Wednesday: 10.00 a.m.–12 noon (partial tour; House of Lords only)
- Thursday: no tours
- Sitting Fridays: 3.30 p.m.–5.00 p.m. (full tour)
- Non-Sitting Fridays: 9.30 a.m.–5.00 p.m. (full tour)

Members' Tours around the estate are open to anyone to book through their MP (many constituents like to take foreign relatives on the tour) but, owing to demand, they have to be booked

56 Monday tours tend to be the most popular because they run for the whole of the morning, meaning constituents aren't as pressured to get to Parliament so early

six months in advance through the Central Tours Office. Making these reservations is, in theory, simple, and is achieved by emailing the Central Tours Office with the following information:

- The surname of one constituent wanting to go on a tour.
- The number of people in their group.
- The date and time they would like to go on a tour.

The Central Tours Office will then provisionally book the group on the most appropriate tour for their requirements and send you a reservation form. This will request the names of all the people in the group and ask for confirmation that the time and date of the tour they've been allocated are suitable. You can either forward this form to the constituents to fill out themselves or call them to ask for the relevant details.

To stand the best chance of getting your constituents on the tour they want, you need to be aware of how the Central Tours Office booking system works. For example, the Central Tours Office will open for bookings at 8.30 a.m. on 1 October for tours that will take place in April the following year, and requests are dealt with on a first-come, first-served basis.

In this case, the trick will be to instruct constituents throughout September to provide dates that they would be able to visit in April. This means that as soon as the clock hits 8.30 a.m. on 1 October, you can send a series of booking requests to the Central Tours Office. Managing requests in this way gives you a very good chance of getting the constituents on the tour they want.

During weekends and recess weeks, these Blue Badge tours continue to take place, but at a cost of £25 per adult and £10 per child. Understandably, many people wishing to visit the Houses of Parliament prefer to book a tour through their MP, which means that most of the weekend and recess-week tours are filled by tourists. However, it is not unknown for some MPs to expect their parliamentary researchers to conduct tours for constituents during weekends, with one staffer required to do this 'about once a month' for their boss's friends or volunteers.

Big Ben Tours

'Being inside the Palace of Westminster, seeing the MPs and the officials going about their daily routine, and then climbing to the top of St Stephen's Tower to stand alongside Big Ben as it chimes 12 noon is a genuine thrill. You really do feel like you are in the middle of one of the world's most iconic buildings and at the very heart of the mother of all parliaments. It is one of those days that you remember for years and years to come.'

GEOFF AND KAY HADWICK, SURREY

To take part in a tour of Big Ben, you must be a UK citizen and aged over thirteen years. These tours only take place on weekdays and, as with the parliamentary estate tours, they are free of charge. Big Ben tours are highly oversubscribed as only twelve people can go on each tour, and tours set off only once every two hours.

Constituents will be met by a guide in the foyer of Portcullis House, escorted through the tunnel that links the building with the Palace of Westminster over the road, and enter the base of Elizabeth Tower. From here they will gradually climb the 334 spiral stone steps, stopping a few times on the way to sit down and hear a bit more of the story of how, why and by whom Big Ben was built. The guide will ensure the tour watches the clock mechanism operate at quarter to the hour, and then be standing, wearing protective ear plugs, next to the Big Ben bell for the turn of the hour.

Tours for Big Ben are booked through the Big Ben Tours Office.

Similar to Members' Tours, making reservations is simple but has to be done many months in advance. Again, all that is needed at the initial booking stage is a short email from you to the Big Ben Tours Office stating the name of the group, how many people are in it and the date and time they would like to go on a tour. Unlike the Members' Tours, all guests on the Big Ben tour have to submit their address to the House authorities in advance of their visit in order for the security officers to carry out background checks.

Access to Elizabeth Tower and Big Ben is severely restricted and only people booked on tours can climb the steps – not even MPs or staffers are able to access the tower without being booked on a tour.

HOW TO HANDLE A MASS LOBBY OF PARLIAMENT

Occasionally a pressure group, charity or trade union will arrange a 'mass lobby' of parliament. For these events, the organisers will encourage as many of their members or supporters as possible to travel to Parliament and request to meet with their MP in Central Lobby (or sometimes in a room they may have managed to book elsewhere inside Parliament). The purpose for organising a mass lobby is that having so many members of the public in Parliament at one time, all for the same cause, shows a strength of support. Mass lobbies also get MPs talking among themselves and their frontbench colleagues about the issue.

If your MP has a constituent taking part in a mass lobby you will want to email or call them before the event to arrange a time to meet. Make a note of their mobile phone number as they will usually be one of hundreds of people so finding them can be tricky. Sometimes you will have many individual constituents taking part in a mass lobby. It would not be a good use of your MP's time to meet them all one-to-one, so ask them in advance if they're happy to join together and meet in a group.

The Fire Brigade's Union was a frequent user of the mass lobby during the 2010–15 parliament as the coalition government sought to change their retirement and pension plans. A couple of times each year Central Lobby and the public gallery in the Commons would be filled with firefighters in high-visibility jackets and yellow helmets. Prior to a mass lobby in 2012, the London branch of the FBU provided a pro-forma email for their members to use, listed the contact details of all London MPs and instructed that requests to meet should be made at least two weeks in advance.[57] Other frequent mass lobby organisers over recent years have been the Campaign for Real Ale (CAMRA), the Palestine Solidarity Campaign, Christian Aid and Friends of the Earth.

HOW TO HANDLE SCHOOL TRIPS

The number of school children visiting Parliament has increased dramatically over recent years. This is in part thanks to initiatives such as the transport subsidy scheme, which covers part of the travel costs for state schools outside London and the south east.

Many of your boss's local schools will organise a trip through the Education Service, which aims to 'Inform, Engage, Empower' by connecting schools and young people with both Houses of Parliament.[58]

Schools that arrange a visit through the Education Service receive a tour around the parliamentary estate, followed by a workshop on the workings of Parliament. Your MP will always be invited to take part in a fifteen-minute Q&A session as part of

57 See www.london.fbu.org.uk/?p=1733

58 See www.parliament.uk/education

this workshop. These invitations are usually issued a couple of months before the school visit, and most MPs will do their best to keep the time available in their diary to see the students. Some MPs will go further and book the meeting room for an extra half-hour in order to spend more time taking questions and explaining to the students how Parliament works.

Your MP is likely to ask you to secure tickets for the pupils to visit the public gallery. While the Admissions Order Office and the doorkeepers prefer not to permit large groups to the gallery, if they are given advance warning of the request they are likely to help out as best they can. Often, to save time checking all the pupils' coats and bags into lockers before they go into the gallery, the doorkeepers will ask you to sit in St Stephen's with the students' possessions.

HOW TO BE GREEN CARDED

Occasionally a constituent will turn up in Parliament unannounced. This technique is referred to as 'green carding' and refers to the Green Card that members of the public can obtain in Central Lobby to request to meet their MP. After the Green Card has been submitted to the reception desk in Central Lobby, it will be given to a doorkeeper who will call your office to inform you there is a constituent wanting to see the MP. MPs are not obliged to meet constituents who Green Card them, though most will do so – but probably after asking you to meet them first to assess the nature of the visit, whether they need to find somewhere private on the estate to talk and how long they should say they can spare to help resolve the issue. You should communicate this information to your MP via text before they come to meet the constituent. If the MP is unable to meet the constituent, you should make notes on the issue of concern and explain that these will be passed on to the MP and the caseworker, who will be able to take up the case.

• • •

YOU WILL SPEND many hours each month explaining to constituents the logistics of visiting Parliament (which tube station to come to, where the entrances to Parliament are) and booking them a place on one of the tours. This process is made more efficient if you have a clear understanding of how the booking system operates, and maintain a list of tour requests that can be emailed to the relevant bookings office as soon as they open each month.

Though this isn't the most exciting aspect of your job, it can be highly rewarding to meet constituents after their tour and hear how much they've enjoyed their visit. It is also important for Parliament itself that more people visit and see for themselves how the place operates.

HOW TO GIVE A TOUR

'Being shown round Parliament by a staffer brings the place to life – you get a real feel for how the system works. Sitting in the Commons, in front of the glass screen, watching PMQs was an interesting and fascinating experience; we were struck by how loud the chamber is with everyone shouting, gossiping and waving papers around. We watched BBC assistant political correspondent, Norman Smith, make his broadcast from the Commons and one of the highlights of the day was lunch in the canteen of Portcullis House and playing "spot the MP".'

CLAIRE AND JOHN, WILTSHIRE

Your work pass allows you to take guests (up to a maximum of six) around all the locations included in the official Members' Tours. While you may not know who is in every picture or when each statue was put in its place, you have the ability to entertain visitors with jokes and tales about the day-to-day workings of Parliament. You can share stories from the mundane to the exceptional and explain what it's like to work and operate according to the building's unique customs. You should also show constituents parts of the estate that the official tours don't cover as this will make them feel that they're receiving 'access-all-areas' treatment. Most constituents are intrigued to meet the parliamentary researcher and keen to understand what your role is and how you operate. Indeed, staffers often find that a constituent's first question isn't about Parliament but 'So what do you do?'

Due to all this, constituents often enjoy tours from a parliamentary researcher just as much as they do with the official Members' Tours, sometimes even more so. There are two big advantages to the MP's office running tours around Parliament, rather than booking constituents on the official tours. The first is that the tours are far easier to organise. Many constituents contact their MP only a couple of weeks before they want to visit – they may be coming down on a family trip to the capital and want to encompass a tour of Parliament in their day. In these circumstances, the availability of official tours will be extremely limited or, more likely, non-existent. Constituents will therefore be extremely grateful when you offer to take time from your day to show them around, and it'll save you a lot of effort going back and forth between constituent and the Central Tours Office trying to find a suitable time.

The second advantage is that staffer-led tours provide an opportunity for you to hear feedback on your MP's performance and their reputation in the constituency. As a parliamentary researcher you are physically and culturally detached from the constituency – your view of politics and the MP's activities from within the Westminster Village mindset is a completely different vantage point from how constituents will see it. Most parliamentary researchers rarely travel to the constituency, so tours are the most frequent opportunities for you to meet people who live in the different towns and village across the constituency. During the time you spend with your guests you can ask questions such as 'How do you think the MP is getting on?' and find out whether they are aware of the MP's latest campaign in their area. Naturally, you will want to steer the conversation to focus on the good work the MP is doing locally.

Some MPs will give tours themselves – though this is a rare act. One MP says, 'It is a foolish underuse of time, and more importantly the energy of an MP, to act routinely as a guide on a tour.'[59] Some MPs, however, will organise a coach to bring forty people down from the constituency. On these occasions, the parliamentary researcher will lead on all the organisation of the coach and promote the availability of the tour across the MP's website, social media and e-newsletter. If the parliamentary researcher has a good relationship with the local newspaper, they might even be able to secure the tour a small story in the next edition.

A cynical view would be that MPs who organise coach trips like this do so for the added bonus that most of the constituents who take part in them are retired (since the trips take place on a weekday). Over-65s, as we know, are far more likely to vote. The more positive view of these tours, however, is that they are genuine attempts by MPs to open up and explain Parliament to their constituents.

Ben Gummer MP, who organises tours for his constituents to make the 170-mile round trip from Ipswich, writes on his website:

> One of the things that worried me before the election, and has become even more obvious since, is how distant Parliament and Westminster seem to most people. This is wrong: it is your Parliament. I want

59 Paul Flynn MP, *How to Be an MP* (London: Biteback Publishing, 2012), p. 152

> to do what I can to help you understand what Parliament does and what I do there as your representative.[60]

Similarly, fellow East-Anglian Conservative MP Brandon Lewis advertised in his *Reporting Back* magazine, of which 35,000 are delivered across his Great Yarmouth constituency, that he organises coach trips for his constituents 'to give them an insight into the everyday workings of this historic building'.[61]

Constituents also organise their own coach trips, with groups such as the local branch of the Women's Institute or Age UK arranging for their members to visit Parliament and go on one of the Members' Tours. In these cases the parliamentary researcher will work with the lead organiser from the group to book a suitable tour and provide practical guidance, such as where is a good place for the bus to drop them close to Parliament's main entrance, or to remind them to leave earlier than they would think necessary to allow time for getting stuck in London's traffic. When your MP has a large group of constituents visiting Parliament they will probably ask you to book a committee room near the Commons chamber so that they can sit down with the constituents and answer questions about what they do in Parliament to represent the area. These sessions will be similar to those they run with local school children who visit Westminster.

If it's a smaller group of constituents visiting your MP will, weather permitting, want to take them out onto the terrace overlooking the Thames for a cup of tea. Access to the terrace is restricted to MPs, Lords and their guests, so constituents will feel very privileged to have had the opportunity to sit there and absorb the grandeur of Parliament from this entirely new perspective.

60 See http://bengummer.com/tour-of-parliament

61 See www.brandonlewis.co/wp-content/uploads/2014/11/2014.11.27-Reporting-Back-Magazine.pdf

HOW TO GET GALLERY TICKETS

Before or after their tour many constituents will appreciate the opportunity to sit in the public gallery of the House of Commons and watch part of a debate. Unless it's Prime Minister's Questions, tickets for the public gallery are fairly easy to get hold of. Usually you can just go up to the Admissions Order Office, which is located off Central Lobby to the west of the Commons entrance, and ask for tickets for use straight away.[62] If there are only a few constituents, ask for tickets to the 'Special Gallery'. While these are still behind the glass screen that separates the public gallery from the chamber, the fact that the ticket has 'Special' written boldly on its front, and the entrance to these seats will take the constituents through the Members' Lobby (rather than the normal public gallery entrance), will give your guests the impression they are receiving superior treatment.[63] You do not need to accompany constituents to the galleries; when they've had enough of watching the MPs below, they will be able to walk out of Parliament through St Stephen's Hall and Westminster Hall.

HOW TO GET PMQ TICKETS

There is a black market for Prime Minister's Questions (PMQs) tickets and only a very small number of parliamentary researchers ever know how to score additional places for their constituents.

---

62 Staffers who are on good terms with the officers who work in the Admissions Order Office do better at this, particularly at times when they have a large group of constituents all wanting to go in the public gallery at the same time. It can be done – but only if the officers and the doorkeepers are willing to help out. If they don't, they will split the group up and give them each only ten minutes in the gallery

63 If their MP is sitting in the Commons chamber a parliamentary researcher would be wise to text them to let them know they have constituents in the public gallery. The constituents will appreciate a wave of acknowledgement and the MP will be grateful for the alert, which will prompt them to be on their best behaviour

Due to the popularity of PMQs, tickets for the public gallery are given to MPs through an allocation list. Each MP is allocated three sets of two tickets per year. For most this is not enough to meet the demand from constituents. An MP will therefore be very grateful to you if you're able to obtain enough extra tickets to ensure that they're not having to say 'no' to any requests.

There are a number of channels through which you can acquire additional PMQ tickets.

1. *Tickets from another MP*

Not all MPs use their allocation, particularly those with far-away constituencies in Northern Ireland, western Wales or northern Scotland. Go through the allocation list, which can be found on the parliamentary intranet, and identify the MPs least likely to be using their tickets. These are the ones you should target first, following these steps:

- Email the MPs least likely to be using their allocation two months before your constituents require the tickets. This email should be sent from your boss's account, and each MP should be sent a message individually and addressed by first name (this is to give the impression the email is coming direct from the MP, not from you). Some staffers choose to make up a bit of a story to the request, such as the constituents are visiting as part of sixtieth birthday celebrations.

- Offer to reciprocate the favour by allowing the MP use of one of your boss's future allocations (though chances are they will never take this up).

- If the MP agrees to this swap, ensure that a member of their staff contacts the Admissions Order Office to confirm to them that the tickets are being passed on to another MP to use.

- These tickets can then be collected from the Admissions Order Office either the day before PMQs or on the day itself. It is advisable to pick up the tickets the day before so that your guests can sign the tickets when you first meet them in Portcullis House, rather than doing it among the crowds later in Central Lobby.

2. *Tickets in front of the security screen*

Many staffers (and many MPs) are unaware that MPs are entitled to two tickets each month in the side galleries that run above the benches of the Commons. These galleries are for members of the House of Lords, personal guests of the Speaker and distinguished visitors, however they are rarely filled to capacity and leftover space is given out to MPs on a first-come, first-served basis. While the views from these galleries is restricted to just one side of the House, the natural noise of a packed House of Commons more than compensates. Constituents will remark about how much chatter and shouting takes place. Hearing PMQs this way, rather than through the filter of the microphones that dangle down into the Commons chamber, will give them a whole new perspective of the event.

- To get tickets in these side galleries the MP has to submit a 'front of screen' request form, which can be downloaded from the parliamentary intranet, in person to the Admissions Order Office. Parliamentary researchers cannot submit requests. As these tickets are given out on a first-come, first-served basis, it is advisable to get the application form in at the earliest possible opportunity. If your boss is in the chamber, text them when you see them leave to remind them to pop in to see the Admissions Order Office.

- This form must include the names and addresses of the guests. The MP needs to sign to confirm that they know the guests and he or she trusts them to behave in front of the security screen by not talking loudly or throwing anything down onto the floor of the House.

- The MP will receive an email to let them know if they have been successful or unsuccessful in securing these tickets.

- If the MP is successful the tickets can be collected either the day before PMQs or on the day itself. As with public gallery tickets, it is advisable to pick up the tickets the day before so that your visitors can sign the tickets in advance of joining the crowds in Central Lobby.

3. Tickets through the whips, the Chairman of Ways and Means and the Commonwealth Office

The whips sometimes have additional tickets that they can hand out to MPs to whom they may owe a favour – or who they want to owe them a favour. Usually it is only the MP who is able to approach the whips to see if they have spare tickets.

The Speaker and the Chairman of Ways and Means (the deputy Speaker) control a weekly allocation of PMQ tickets reserved for any distinguished guests they may be entertaining. Sometimes they do not pass any spares on to the Admissions Order Office so it's worthwhile getting on friendly terms with their staffers so that you can contact them direct. Finally, the Commonwealth Office also has a similar allocation for any guests they may have in Parliament. They too can be contacted direct to request any tickets they may not be using.

4. Try your luck on the day

If you and your MP have tried all of these options and are still unable to get tickets it is still worth ringing the Admissions Order Office on the morning of PMQs to check if there have been any cancellations or if any tickets have been handed back at the last minute. In theory, any spare tickets are released at 11 a.m. but those on good terms with the Admissions Order Office can usually call earlier in the day. If an MP is desperate to get tickets they can visit the Admissions Order Office themselves and they will get priority.

HOW TO ENSURE YOUR GUESTS LOVE THEIR DAY

Access to the House of Commons closes ninety minutes prior to it sitting. This is to allow for sniffer dogs to walk through the benches and various other security checks to be carried out. This means that if constituents want to stand on the floor of the chamber and touch the Despatch Boxes before PMQs they need to be in Parliament by 9.30 a.m.[64] You will then have the task of entertaining them for two hours before PMQs starts.

Fortunately, most constituents tend to prefer getting the quieter and cheaper trains that arrive in London after rush hour. The ideal time for them to arrive is 10.30 a.m. as this allows for a fifty-minute tour through Westminster Hall, St Stephen's, the Chapel of St Mary Undercroft and the House of Lords. Time the tour well and you will get a good place to stand in Central Lobby to watch the Speaker's Procession, which takes place just before the House of Commons sits (the best spot is near the exit

64 The House of Commons sits at 11.30 a.m. on Wednesdays

that leads to the public galleries, as this improves the chance of your constituents getting good seats).

Many MPs will meet their constituents after PMQs and take them for lunch in one of Parliament's canteens or, if it's sunny, on the terrace overlooking the Thames. Constituents tend to really enjoy this opportunity to speak to their MP and you and to learn more about the work you both do in Westminster. The MP will want to spend just enough time with their guests to make them feel duly attended to, but not too long in case they get the impression that they aren't busy enough.

When lunch is over you should complete the tour by taking the constituents up onto the roof of the House of Commons, through the ministerial car park and finally to one of the exits to say your goodbyes.

If you and your boss can execute all these tasks smoothly then chances are you will have given your guests a day they will remember for many years, and tell many people about back in the constituency.

Chapter 6

Using Parliament

A STRATEGIC USE OF Oral and Written Questions, followed up by an Adjournment or Westminster Debate and even a Private Member's Bill, accompanied by a proactive media and digital strategy, can successfully demonstrate to a government minister an MP's determination to campaign on an issue.

HOW TO USE QUESTIONS

MPs ask thousands of Parliamentary Questions (PQs) every year. Used effectively they can be a valuable tool for scrutinising the work of government departments and obtaining information ministers either haven't thought to release into the public domain or, most likely, don't want to. Used ineffectively, PQs waste a lot of civil service time and cost a lot of money; each Written Parliamentary Question costs £149 to be answered, Oral ones are £410 each.

There are three types of Parliamentary Questions:

1. Oral: Oral Questions are asked by MPs on the floor of the House direct to the secretary of state and his or her ministers. Limited time in the Commons schedule means not all Oral Questions on the Order Paper can be answered.

2. Written: Written Questions are answered by a minister with a written answer sent to the MP. There is no time limit imposed on the government to answer these, but MPs expect to receive a reply within two weeks and the Speaker encourages ministers to ensure that responses are 'timely'.

3. Written for Named Day: Written for Named Day Questions are used when the MP needs an answer fast. A minister must reply by a specified date (three days or more later). An answer is guaranteed, but how substantive this answer is depends on the ease with which the information can be collected. If the information is not easy to collect the minister may send a 'holding' answer before responding thoroughly a few days or weeks (or sometimes months) later.

PQs are similar to Freedom of Information requests in that their role is to obtain information from the government, not to make a point or pass an opinion. The website w4mp.org has outlined a number of points for you to keep in mind when drafting a PQ:[65]

- It must not be biased – your language needs to be neutral. For example, if you table a Question using the word 'failure', this is

65 See www.w4mp.org/library/guides/parliament-guides/how-it-works/parliamentary-questions-pqs

accusing the government. The Table Office will remove it and change it to 'performance' or something similar.

- It must not convey information or construct an argument. So you shouldn't say, '100 people in my constituency have written to me about rabbit welfare, doesn't the government need to act?'

- It must not seek opinion – only information. You may draft around this, however. Instead of asking what a minister thinks of something, you may ask 'what assessment he/she has made', or 'what estimate he/she has made'. You can also add 'and if (s) he will make a statement' at the end, if you are seeking further general ministerial comment.

- Keep language simple and the Question concise; use the minimum number of words and do not use words that are too descriptive. For example, most Questions asking a minister what 'action' or 'measures' he/she is taking will be changed to 'steps'.

- There must be a basis for the Question – it must not be based solely on, for example, newspaper speculation.

- It must not ask for information for which that department is not responsible – check you've got the right department, and that the issue is not the responsibility of one of the devolved administrations.

- Check that the Question hasn't already been asked and answered recently.

- Check that the information isn't blocked by, for example, discussions taking place during Cabinet meetings, which are not obliged to be disclosed.

- Be careful of asking for information which would be considered *sub judice* to provide (information which would prejudice a court case). In a PQ, you cannot make reference to an active court case. A case is considered active in a criminal court when a charge has been made and in a civil court when the case has been 'set down' for trial.

Questions can be submitted to the Table Office (known as 'tabling') and, as long as the writing is legible and the Question has been signed by the MP, then it could be tabled on the back of a cigarette packet or an old receipt. Most MPs today prefer to table Questions electronically (known as 'e-tabling') and the e-tabling app can be installed on your laptop so that you can submit Questions on behalf of your boss.

Oral Questions

Each day (except Fridays) the House of Commons begins with an hour of departmental Oral Questions. These operate on a rota that sees each department take its turn once every five sitting weeks. In these sessions, the secretary of state and his or her ministers must do their best to provide answers (or cleverly construct non-answers) to the Questions put to them by backbench MPs and shadow ministers.

Questions must be drafted and submitted to the Table Office three sitting days before the relevant Question session takes place. This is to allow the ministers, their Spads and civil servants time to prepare responses and practise any key lines. All Questions go into a ballot, with MPs drawn out at random. First in the ballot is first on the Order Paper. For each Questions session about fifteen MPs will be given a place on the Order Paper, though MPs not down to ask a Question may still go into the chamber to 'bob' (when MPs stand up and down in between

Questions) at the Speaker. The Speaker will call on bobbing MPs to even up the distribution of Questions. If the Conservative Party have two backbench MPs drawn together on the Order Paper, the Speaker may call a member of the SNP or Liberal Democrats to ask a Question.

Due to the tabling regulations, Oral Questions appear quite bland at first. For example, 'What plans does the government have to support investment in school buildings?' was asked by Pudsey MP Andrew Stephenson during Education Questions on 15 June 2015. However, after the minister's first response to the Question on the Order Paper, all the rules for the drafting of Questions go out the window as backbenchers ask their 'supplementary' Question. Supplementaries are generally used by opposition MPs to attack and attempt to wrong-foot the minister while firing up their own backbenchers. Government MPs seek to do the exact opposite. Their supplementary Question will seek to lay up the perfect pass for the minister to promote the government's work, congratulate the MP on the fantastic work he or she is doing in the constituency, or slam home a jibe at the party opposite. If tabled Questions are about obtaining information, supplementaries are mainly used for political point-scoring.

Some MPs do use their tabled and supplementary Questions to highlight a pressing local issue: a local business park may be struggling with exceptionally poor broadband services or a number of road accidents may have taken place at a busy roundabout in the area. In the case of Andrew Stephenson MP, his supplementary Question asked: 'Colne Park high school is in desperate need of funds to improve the state of its building, but it is receiving inadequate support from the local county council. Will my hon. friend consider meeting the school's leadership team to help to find a way forward?' To which the minister, Sam Gyimah MP, responded:

> I appreciate that the school will be disappointed that its application

> to the second phase of the Priority School Building programme was unsuccessful. The programme was highly over-subscribed, and we had to prioritise the buildings in the worst condition. However, Lancashire's indicative allocation to maintain and improve its schools is £34 million for 2015–18, and I expect it to consider carefully the needs of all schools in its area. I will do what I can to support my hon. friend with that.

This one-two tactic can be highly effective in bringing matters to the attention of the government and securing a meeting with a minister. Your MP will expect you to have watched their Question on TV and will want you to quickly share the news of the government's response on their social media and, if you believe necessary, issue a press release to local newspaper and radio journalists.

Written Questions

Graham Jones (Lab, Hyndburn): To ask the Secretary of State for Health what the average waiting time is for mental health talking therapies in (a) England, (b) the North West, (c) East Lancashire and (d) Hyndburn constituency.

WRITTEN QUESTION, 24 FEBRUARY 2015

Paul Flynn writes that the purpose of Written Questions is to:

- Put pressure on government to act.
- Necklace the Executive with ineradicable comments.
- Reveal opponents' inactivity/neglect/stupidity.
- Advertise and strengthen campaigns with authoritative official facts.

- Induce non-replies that expose government evasiveness.
- Highlight the MP's constituency.
- Seek facts and bring them into the public domain.[66]

Parliamentary researchers who are skilful in the drafting of Written Questions find them an effective weapon in extracting useful information out of the government. In the example of Graham Jones MP (above), he is looking to find out how his constituency and region compare to national standards. If the local average waiting times are worse than the national average then he can use this as his angle to launch a campaign and attack the government.

In the 2014 Autumn Statement the coalition government made a number of announcements for road improvement schemes as part of the Department for Transport's road investment strategy. Many of the improvements announced were in marginal constituencies and would, therefore, have given positive news coverage for coalition MPs and candidates. Written Questions tabled immediately after the Autumn Statement, which probed deeper into the Department for Transport's road investment strategy, revealed a lack of substance behind the government's announcements. It turned out that money was not being made available for all the projects, instead many would only be having a study to see if funding should be allocated for the project to go ahead sometime between 2020 and 2025. The answers from these Written Questions were then able to be used by opposition MPs to challenge the government's claims both in Parliament and in the press.

At the back of your mind you should always be thinking of ideas for Written Questions that your boss can table. MPs can submit as many Written Questions as they like (however only five can

66 Paul Flynn, *How to Be an MP*, p. 55

be tabled each day through the e-tabling app). TheyWorkForYou rates MPs by how many Written Questions they ask and this means most MPs will want you to be drafting sufficient Questions to ensure they look busy and active. One government minister, when she was a backbencher seeking to impress her superiors, ordered her parliamentary researcher to prioritise the drafting of five Written Questions a day so that she could remain at the top of the TheyWorkForYou rankings.

Charities, businesses, lobbyists and pressure groups will always be happy to assist with the drafting of Written Questions. You should also speak regularly with the constituency staffers to see if they have any ideas for Questions. The final place to seek inspiration for Questions is to look through those that other MPs have recently tabled to see if any of them can be changed slightly and re-submitted. Taking the example of the Written Question from Graham Jones MP, his request for data about the North West, East Lancashire and Hyndburn could be changed to a different constituency in a different region.

The main obstacle you'll face when seeking to table a series of Written Questions is getting them through the Table Office clerks. The clerks are strict adherers to correct parliamentary language and protocol. If they have any problems with a Question it will be 'carded' and they will call, email or send a card in the post asking to discuss the Question and how it can be changed to meet the submission rules. If you think your Questions have a good chance of being carded, you're better off sending them to the Table Office as a draft version, rather than submitting them officially and hoping they'll go unchecked. Sometimes the clerks are happy just to be given a description of the Question you want to ask. In both cases, they will happily re-draft the Question in perfect parliamentary language ready to be submitted.

Once a Written Question has made it through the Table Office clerks, it will be sent to the relevant department to be answered.

Civil servants will usually draft answers for their minister, however responses to politically difficult Questions, such as 'How much money has the department spent on first-class rail tickets in the last twelve months?' are likely to be drafted by the minister's Spads.

Each Written Question, and the subsequent response from the minister, used to be published each day in the Questions Book. This was stopped in 2014 in order to save Parliament an estimated £795,000 a year. Today the quickest way to keep track of Written Questions is the parliament.uk website, or alerts can be set on TheyWorkForYou that will deliver you a daily digest of a particular department or minister's activities in Parliament over the last twenty-four hours.

HOW TO USE EARLY DAY MOTIONS

Early Day Motions (EDMs) can be thought of as petitions that only MPs can sign. About 2,000 EDMs are tabled in each parliamentary session (in the 1950s there were about 100 a year). The process of tabling an EDM is the same as for Questions and they can be tabled by any MP, though tradition dictates that ministers or shadow ministers only table or sign an EDM if it is of vital importance to their constituency. All EDMs begin with the words 'That this House...'

EDMs tabled in the first weeks of the 2015–16 parliamentary session included:

Fifa Women's World Cup

That this House congratulates Liverpool and Nigerian footballer Asisat Oshoala who is the first player to win the new BBC World Service award, Women's Footballer of the Year; recognises the important role she plays as an ambassador for women's football,

Nigerian football, and Liverpool Football Club; commends the BBC for supporting the women's game and providing full coverage of the upcoming Women's World Cup; and looks forward to the growing success and profile of the BBC's award in future years.

Air Passenger Duty

That this House recognises the economic importance attached to reduced air passenger duty (APD); notes the recent decision by the government of the Irish Republic to sell its stake in Aer Lingus to AIG, British Airways' parent company; acknowledges that this commercial decision could place Dublin as a major hub airport within these islands, with its added advantage of lower Irish APD, thus impacting on longer haul destinations by all other large airports throughout the UK; and calls on the Chancellor of the Exchequer to recognise the massive potential business, tourism and financial loss which this development entails and reduce APD accordingly at the earliest opportunity.

Yulin Dog Meat Festival 2015

That this House condemns the plans to go ahead with the Yulin Dog Meat Festival 2015 in Yulin, China; expresses deep concern at the cruel and inhumane manner in which dogs have been slaughtered in the past; notes the terrible conditions that dogs face prior to being killed as they are held in overcrowded cages without water; and urges the Chinese authorities to intercede to stop the festival from taking place.

Some EDMs are sponsored and written by an outside body, such as a charity or pressure group, and tabled by a pliant MP. The charity or pressure group will then rally their supporters across the country to lobby their local MP to sign the EDM.

HOW TO USE ADJOURNMENT AND WESTMINSTER HALL DEBATES

Adjournment debates are led by backbench MPs and take place in the last half-hour of a sitting day (except on Fridays) before the House adjourns until the next morning. Since 1999, the Grand Committee room off Westminster Hall has been made available as a 'parallel chamber' for backbench-led debates to take place during the daytime. Westminster Hall debates take place 9.30 a.m.–2 p.m. on Tuesday and on Wednesdays from 9.30 a.m. to 11.30 a.m., then from 2.30 p.m. to 5 p.m.

As with Oral Questions, an MP must submit their application for an Adjournment or Westminster Hall debate into a ballot. Subjects debated vary enormously, from ones that will attract the attention of many MPs, such as food waste or sustainable development goals, to ones that attract the attention of much lobbying from constituents, such as nuclear power. Some MPs will apply for an Adjournment debate on a constituency-specific issue, such as 'prisons on the Isle of Sheppey' tabled by Gordon Henderson MP. For these debates, the MP is likely to find themselves to be the only person in the chamber, except for the minister responsible for responding to them. Securing a Westminster Hall debate presents an MP with an opportunity to issue a press release, gain media coverage and rally some support on social media. Mr Henderson MP, for example, gained coverage on ITV Meridian (his regional ITV news) for his debate on local prisons. You might want to consider recording the speech and uploading the video to your MP's website and Facebook page. Finally, if the Adjournment or Westminster debate relates to issues raised by constituents through a survey or community campaign, you or a member of the local team should arrange for the MP to write to everyone who participated in this to let them know he or she has raised their concerns during a special debate in Parliament. Depending on the number of people involved, you may also decide to send them an official copy of Hansard too.

HOW TO USE TEN MINUTE RULE BILLS AND PRIVATE MEMBERS' BILLS

Ten Minute Rule Bills and Private Members' Bills are pretty much the same – both are opportunities for backbench MPs to bring forward new legislation. The major difference is when they are allocated time in the House. Ten Minute Rule Bills give a backbencher a platform to speak, unsurprisingly for ten minutes, in the House of Commons after Question Time on a Tuesday, or after PMQs on a Wednesday. At both of these times the chamber is likely to be reasonably full.

A Private Member's Bill is not guaranteed to receive any debate in the House of Commons. These Bills have a quirky story for how they come to exist. The Private Members' Bills that have the best chance of getting debating time are the 'Ballot Bills'. Being first in the draw, according to Andrew George who came first in the 2014 ballot, is 'the MPs' equivalent of winning the jackpot in the national lottery'.[67]

Each year all backbench MPs place their name into a ballot that is held on the second sitting Thursday of a parliamentary session. Twenty names are drawn in the ballot, with the first seven normally guaranteed to receive a day's debate on their chosen Bill. In the 2014–15 parliamentary session, seven 'Ballot Bills' became law.

- Control of Horses Act 2015

67 See www.falmouthpacket.co.uk/news/11277355.Andrew_George_wins_MPs____equivalent_of_National_Lottery_jackpot/?ref=mry

- Health and Social Care (Safety and Quality) Act 2015
- Health Service Commissioner for England (Complaint Handling) Act 2015
- International Development (Official Development Assistance Target) Act 2015
- Local Government (Religious etc. Observances) Act 2015
- Local Government (Review of Decisions) Act 2015
- Self-build and Custom Housebuilding Act 2015

For those MPs who are not drawn in the ballot, but really want to table a Private Member's Bill, they have the option of queuing outside the Private Member's Bill office three weeks after the ballot. Queuing can begin days in advance. In his documentary for the BBC, *Inside the Commons*, Michael Cockerell filmed then Labour MP Thomas Docherty as he slept for two nights outside the office of Kate Emms, the clerk in charge of Private Members' Bills.

The majority of Ten Minute Rule Bills and Private Members' Bills fail to become law. MPs, though, still choose to pursue them because these Bills can be powerful vehicles on which to campaign for or against a pressing local or national issue.

If your MP wants to table one of these Bills you will need to work with the Private Member's Bill office to ensure the wording of the Bill is in correct parliamentary language (however, not all MPs actually publish a printed Bill). If they're successful you will be required to draft a speech and press release (depending on the issue this may need to go to lobby reporters too). You should also use the MP's website and social media to build support for the Bill from constituents (and relevant charities, businesses and pressure groups if it's a national issue). A good way of doing this is to ask constituents to 'co-sign' the Bill. To do this:

- Post an introduction to the Bill on the MP's website, explaining why the MP believes it is important for their constituency. You may want to include a link to the official version of the Bill on parliament.uk, or upload into your boss's website.

- Offer constituents a simple 'co-sign my Bill' button. This would require constituents to submit their name, postcode and email address.

- Use the MP's e-newsletter and social media (possibly including paying for some adverts) to promote the action, as well as asking constituents to share the Bill on their own social media. For example, a Facebook post or Twitter message could say: 'I want to give every UK citizen £1,000. Show you support this by co-signing my Bill and then share this message [link to a page on MP's website].'

Asking constituents to co-sign a Bill and demonstrate their support for it on social media helps to get the word out about the MP's work, as well as collecting lots of email addresses. To complete the engagement, after the fate of the Bill has been decided, the MP should write back to all co-signers of the Bill to thank them for showing their backing, and to let them know whether or not the Bill was successful.

• • •

THE GOVERNMENT WILL notice an MP's persistent raising of an issue through these different devices and will often take action as a result. In 2013, Andy Sawford MP tabled a number of Written

Questions and introduced a Private Member's Bill that aimed to tackle the exploitative use of zero-hours contracts. While not making it into the statute book, the Bill forced the issue onto the government's (and the national media's) agenda and also helped to bring stories of abusive zero-hours employers to national prominence. The government first responded by asking the Office of National Statistics to change the way it calculated the number of people on these contracts, which revealed that hundreds of thousands more people were on zero-hours contracts than previously officially recognised. This led to a lengthy consultation that highlighted a number of legislative changes that needed to be made to offer greater protection to workers. Some of these have now made it into law.

HOW TO WRITE A SPEECH

Speeches delivered by MPs in the House of Commons or Westminster Hall are very rarely oratorical masterpieces. They are often dense, factual and quite technical. Regardless of how many other MPs are in the chamber, the speech is targeted at just two people – the minister sitting behind the Despatch Box and the Hansard stenographer perched in the Press Gallery above the Speaker's chair. It is unlikely that any local news reporters or constituents will be watching the speech (although some MPs will give an upcoming speech a plug on Twitter and Facebook) so the purpose of the speech is not to entertain, but to get as much content and information as possible down on the official record.

The Hansard copy of the speech becomes the basis for press releases, such as 'MP calls on government to launch inquiry into local schools' or 'MP praises local schools'. If the content of the speech is particularly newsworthy – it may, for example, relate to a highly controversial case of malpractice at a local hospital – this will usually secure the MP an interview on their regional radio and TV news.

You should seek to maximise the reach of the speech by pushing it out across the MP's digital channels. Web tools such as Screencastify can be used to record live TV (or replays on Parliament TV or BBC iPlayer), which can then be uploaded to the MP's website or direct onto Facebook or Twitter as 'native video'. Thanks to 'likes', 'shares', 'retweets' and 'favourites', social media creates the opportunity for the video's reach to grow exponentially among constituents.

Before this stage, though, there are some key things to consider when preparing a speech for your boss:

1 Time: How long is the MP likely to be given to make their speech? If they have secured an Adjournment debate or Westminster Hall debate they will make the opening speech. If it's on quite a niche subject, such as the fiftieth anniversary of a local hero's death, or the re-opening of a popular local park, they will probably get a full fifteen minutes. If, however, the MP is a fairly new backbencher wanting to speak in the debate following the Budget or Queen's Speech, they could end up sitting in the Commons for a whole day only to be given two minutes right at the very end.

2 Flexibility: Because you can never be sure exactly how much time the MP will be given, a speech should be drafted in a way that enables them to adapt it at the last minute. Rather than attempting to construct eloquent prose, you should, at first, write short and sharp. Each page should be a different section, such as: Introduction; Pros; Cons; Local angle; Case study; Calls for action; Conclusion. This will allow the MP to quickly and easily rearrange the order of the speaking notes, or drop whole sections entirely if they don't have enough time.

3 Finding information: The House of Commons Library is staffed by expert research officers who are able to gather pretty much any information you may need. They can find relevant research papers, speeches or anything else that may be useful. You may also want to make contact with relevant pressure groups, charities or lobbyists who might have views on the subject and might be able to provide you with a briefing. The constituency office will be able to identify any local angles or relevant case studies that can be added to the speaking notes.

4 Don't seek perfection: Most speeches are prepared fewer than forty-eight hours before the MP delivers them and it's likely you'll already have a number of other jobs planned during this time. It's better the MP has all the information in note form rather than just a nicely written introduction. Your first job is to pull together all the relevant information you've found and break it up into individual sections on individual pages.

5 Time in the chamber: The MP may have to sit and wait in the chamber for hours before it is their turn to speak. It is in this time that they can go through the notes you've prepared and turn them into a final draft.

6 Presentation: An MP will want to make handwritten comments next to the text. Speaking notes should be printed with double spacing to provide enough room for this. Notes should also be printed twice, with page numbers, to allow for corrections or in case any pages get lost or fall out of sync.

7 Prepare to run: The use of mobile phones and iPads by MPs in the chamber means it is very rare that you'll have to deliver notes to your boss. However, while waiting for their turn to speak, an MP may do some research of their own and find reports or press

statements they'd like to add into their speech. If they want a physical copy of this, you will be required to print one off, run to the chamber and place the documents in a sealed envelope with the MP's name on. This envelope needs to be handed to a doorkeeper, who will then walk it into the chamber and pass it to the MP.

8. Watch on TV: MPs are keen to hear feedback on how they delivered the speech and dealt with interventions and hecklers. It's also nice to hear your hard work being read out in the House of Commons.

9. Get the word out: If the MP is leading an Adjournment or Westminster Hall debate, they can reliably inform constituents what time they will be speaking, so many will post on Twitter and Facebook beforehand to encourage people to watch. After the speech, you should quickly upload a video to the MP's website and social media channels and send a copy of the text to the local media as part of a press release.

10. Send copies of Hansard: If the speech praises a local school or raises the case of a local constituent, it is nice to send them a copy of Hansard, accompanied by a handwritten note from the MP. These can be collected from any vote office. Some parliamentary researchers also collect Hansards in which their boss has made a significant speech.

HOW TO RUN AN ALL PARTY PARLIAMENTARY GROUP

by Emma Darkins, External Relations Officer at the MS Society, and former parliamentary researcher to Heather Wheeler MP, chair of the local government APPG.

An All Party Parliamentary Group (APPG) does not have any power to make laws and is not funded by Parliament. An APPG will have one of three purposes:

1. To foster links with other countries. There is an APPG for most countries of the world.
2. To address a particular issue. The APPG I was involved in, the APPG for local government, carried out an investigation into social care, for example.
3. Some APPGs exist for social reasons, such as the APPGs on basketball, running and Weight Watchers.

Working for an MP who is the chair of an APPG means you have to be organised. Most APPGs have professional bodies to support them – for example, the APPG for local government is supported by the Local Government Information Unit. It is the professional secretariat's role to work to set the agenda for the APPG alongside its parliamentary members, but it will be your role to ensure that the infrastructure is in place for the APPG activity to happen.

Although an APPG is not a formal working group within Parliament its activity is overseen by the Committee on Standards. Key requirements of an APPG include:

- Making and maintaining a register entry.
- Admitting members and electing officers – the group must have at least four officers.
- Each group must meet at least twice during its reporting year.
- Formal meetings (which involve the group making one or more decision) must be published in the All Party Notice.

- Groups must be transparent about their nature, membership and funding.

One thing you must ensure is that the register is kept up to date. Any updates must come from the chair of the group's office and not the secretariat. To do this successfully you must liaise regularly with the group's secretariat and ensure that you keep an up-to-date record of the APPG's activity.

You also have to ensure that the APPG meetings are published in the All Party Notice. This is sent round by email on Thursdays to all parliamentarians. To ensure that your meeting gets into the notice you have to notify the All Party Notice team at the latest by close of play the day before the notice goes out (so this would currently be a Wednesday).

However, the major part of your role will be to ensure that the APPG has meeting rooms booked at appropriate times for its members and the secretariat. Booking meeting rooms in Parliament can be a challenge, especially if you're aiming for a committee room when parliament is in full swing.

My biggest piece of advice is to make sure you have a good relationship with the House of Commons events team – you will be calling them a lot! All room bookings in Parliament must be made through them. When booking a committee room for APPG business be sure to avoid Monday mornings, Thursday afternoons and Fridays as MPs are often heading in from or back to their constituencies at these times. Also be clear of numbers for your meeting before calling the events team, they will always ask for this information and try to fit you into the room that best fits your requirements. If you want the room for longer than two hours then you will need another MP to sponsor the room with you. If this is the case ask the office of an MP who is attending your meeting if they mind you putting their name down as a second sponsor.

If you book one of the committee rooms for your APPG event

and you find you get a good spot on a Tuesday or Wednesday – be prepared, you may get 'bumped'. The events team have a duty to make sure that committee rooms are available for select committees and they get priority – even if you did book the room months in advance. However, the events team are excellent in letting you know as soon as they do and working with you to find an alternative room. This happens often, so be prepared to let your members and secretariat know as soon as it does.

HOW TO DEAL WITH A BILL

by Grace Wright, senior parliamentary researcher

This chapter applies primarily to parliamentary researchers working for the opposition. When the government introduces a new piece of legislation (known as a 'Bill') into Parliament, the shadow minister with responsibility for that area takes the lead on responding to it for the opposition. This means everything from leading for the opposition in debates, to drafting amendments and managing the press.

As a parliamentary researcher for a shadow minister, you may have the opportunity to manage a Bill. To put this into context – the government minister in charge of the Bill will have an entire Civil Service department supporting her or him. Your boss will have you. The workload is intense and parliamentary researchers managing Bills generally work all hours and miss pleasantries like lunch and sleep. It is, though, one of the best experiences you can have in the job.

The basics

A Bill can be introduced into either the Commons or Lords first. It goes through the same five stages of debate in both Houses

– First Reading, Second Reading, Committee Stage, Report Stage and Third Reading. This is followed by a quick-fire round called 'Ping-Pong' (that is its official name), in which the Bill 'pings' between the two Houses until they have each agreed the other's amendments.

There are three key things to do when you hear you have got a Bill:

1. Go and pick up a copy of the Bill and the explanatory notes. Write your name, clearly, at the top of your copy. This is your master copy. You will fill it with indispensably valuable notes about what needs amending, and then your boss will inevitably try to wander off with it. Put your name on it.

2. Read the Bill. Read the explanatory notes, figure out what the Bill does and write yourself a summary of each clause. This summary document will be the best reference point you have while you're trying to introduce people to the Bill and know what you're talking about. Give copies to your MP, the rest of your ministerial team and anyone else who needs one.

3. Go and introduce yourself to the Public Bill Office (PBO). They are a friendly, endlessly patient office who will help you table and draft amendments and kindly answer all the other questions you have. Your MP needs to formally 'introduce' you to the PBO, so get your boss to walk up there with you as soon as you know there is a Bill coming your way.

Preparation

Once you've done these things, you're ready to staff a Bill.

The next step is 'strategy'. Your MP (and you) will have strategy meetings with ministerial colleagues to decide what you support in the Bill, what you wholeheartedly oppose, what is missing from the Bill and what needs changing. These changes will form the list of amendments that you eventually put down.

You will also be asked to set up meetings with outside experts, charities, businesses and other groups that have expertise in that policy area. These groups will come forward with concerns and campaigns, and can provide support with relevant data, case studies and help with drafting amendments.

Now come the debates. First Reading is a formality – all that happens is the title of the Bill is announced in the chamber and a date is declared for Second Reading.

Second Reading is the first debate you have on a Bill. It happens in the House of Commons chamber ('on the floor of the House') and all MPs are allowed to take part.

The debate starts with 'opening speeches' from government and opposition ministers, which set out why the government is introducing the Bill and what the opposition position is, and finishes with closing arguments (known as 'wind ups') from both sides.

The most important thing about Second Reading is that it is a general debate. Your boss will be asked to make either the opening or closing speech – most likely the closing. This speech needs to talk about the Bill in its entirety: what we welcome, what we don't and what we are looking forward to polishing up or pulling apart in future debates. You don't put down your amendments at Second Reading. The detailed debate and amendments come next.

Committee Stage

Committee Stage is the heavy lifting. On an average-to-long Bill, you will write what feels like hundreds of speeches and amendments. You may find yourself longing for simple things like a nine-to-five job or the outdoors. But you will also become an expert on your Bill and be genuinely indispensable to your team.

A Public Bill Committee is formed with representative numbers of MPs from the government, the opposition and the smaller parties. Your boss will be the 'lead member' for the opposition. The committee sits for a number of days, over a number of weeks, and debates every clause and every suggested amendment.

- There are different types of amendment. You can write an amendment to an existing clause or schedule, or you can table a 'New Clause' that you want adding to the Bill.

- Amendments (including new clauses) have to be within the 'scope' of the Bill. This means they have to be directly related to what the Bill is about. For example, you can't put down an amendment about vaccinating badgers onto a Bill about banking.

- The Public Bill Office (PBO) are there to help. Go and ask them, whatever the question. There will be an individual PBO clerk allocated specifically to your Bill.

- There are deadlines for when you have to table an amendment by, ahead of each committee session. Get your amendments checked by the PBO well in advance of the deadline.

- Making a speech on an amendment is called 'speaking to' that amendment. During the committee sessions, your boss will be called on to speak to every amendment you put down. These speeches are to convince the committee that they should vote to make the change you've suggested.

- The best tip I can give is – keep an eye on what other people are doing. The government and other committee members will put down amendments, and your boss will also have to speak to these to set out the opposition view. Check the published list of amendments every day.

- The committee usually starts with Clause 1, and continues through the Bill debating amendments along the way. The committee isn't timetabled to debate a set number of clauses in each session – they just start where they left off and get through as much as they can. Don't risk them reaching a clause or group of amendments that your MP isn't prepared for – prepare speeches on extra clauses in advance.

Report Stage

At this point, you will all be delighted that Committee Stage is over. Report Stage is the big showdown. The Bill comes out of committee and returns to the floor of the Commons.

At Report Stage, your team pick the top few issues that you want to debate and table amendments on those only (usually four or five big amendments). These are then debated and, if desired, voted on by the whole House. As ever, check with the PBO what you can and can't table. This stage is usually timetabled to take up one or two afternoons in the chamber.

Over both Committee and Report Stage, it is relatively rare for the opposition to get a big win and either defeat the government on a vote or convince the government to change their policy. With that said, it does happen. If you manage to get an amendment accepted, be proud. Maybe even get the amendment paper framed, with a caption that reads 'proof I changed the law'. How you celebrate is really up to you.

Third Reading

When you reach Third Reading, the end is in sight. This is the wind-up debate and is usually tacked on to the end of Report Stage as the final hour of business in the chamber. This is another general debate, used to summarise earlier arguments, make threats about future amendments in the House of Lords or congratulate members who have improved the Bill.

• • •

THIS IS A quick summary of the Bill process, so there are inevitably exceptions to the rules laid out here and details that we haven't been able to include. The Public Bill Office run informal training sessions for members and their staff, just pop up and ask to book one.

After Third Reading you will either be required to help your Lords team as they work on the Bill in the House of Lords, or be ready for 'ping-pong'. 'Ping-pong' can require some work and it can happen quickly. Make sure you ask the PBO clerks to explain the process ahead of time.

And, at the end of it all, ask for some time off. Enjoy.

Chapter 7

The media

HOW TO WORK WITH YOUR LOCAL MEDIA

BEFORE YOU CAN build an effective relationship with the reporters who regularly report on their MP, you must first know who they are. Most offices should have a database of local journalists, who they work for, what their role is and their contact details. To be really successful in dealing with the media you should put in the work to build personal relationships of shared trust and respect with these reporters.

The best way of achieving this is to meet them in person. Each regional TV news broadcaster will have one reporter based in Westminster whose primary focus is to cover the activities of MPs from their patch when they are in the House of Commons. For the local radio and newspaper journalists based in the constituency, you can build relationships by regularly talking to them over the phone, or arranging to meet them on the first occasion they visit the local office. Sometimes it is possible to invite local reporters to Westminster. This could be to report on a significant event, such as a meeting with the health secretary that confirms a large investment in GP services in the constituency; the chance to watch PMQs or even to meet the Prime Minister at Downing Street, just as Conservative MPs and candidates invited local newspaper editors to do in 2014.

You will want to know how each journalist operates. What are their deadlines for filing stories? What type of stories do they prefer? Parliamentary process or human interests? What is the best way to communicate with them? Via phone call or text? You should come to develop an understanding of the following things:

- Who will be most interested in which stories? It would be a waste of time to offer a reporter an exclusive about the MP's work in the European Union select committee if they're more interested in telling the stories of the human impact of the government's welfare policies.

- What is the most effective way of informing a reporter of a story? There is no point sending out a press release late on a Wednesday afternoon if the paper has gone to press earlier that morning. Equally, if a TV reporter is happy to take up an exclusive story from a phone call there is no need to write a 400-word press release.

- What are the party's lines on this issue? Most MPs will usually want to relate their comment in the media to the party's front-bench policy. This can be done either by checking recent frontbench briefings, calling the Spads of the relevant party spokesperson or calling the party's media team at HQ.

If you show appreciation for a journalist's deadlines and the pressures they are working under, then they will be more likely to invite your MP to provide interviews and quotes for their stories.

HOW TO WRITE A PRESS RELEASE

> Your local media is arguably more important to your boss's re-election hopes than the most prominent article in the nationals ... For this reason, it's always worth developing a good relationship with the hacks at your local rag, not least because if you take them seriously, they will take you seriously and maybe even tip you off as to upcoming issues in your member's patch and come to you first for quotes and comments.[68]

The reality of today's local media industry, particularly the print media, is that fewer journalists are being required to publish more stories, for less money. Use this to your advantage; write a good press release, send it within the reporters' deadlines and it's almost guaranteed to be copied, pasted and published just the way you want it to be.

Below are some simple steps on how to write an effective press release:

1. Send it out at a good time of day (and of the week). Send the press release too early and it may get lost in all the other emails and spam the reporter will have received overnight. Send it too late and the reporter may already have agreed their stories for the day with their editor and will be busy sourcing interviews and writing them up. Between 9 and 10 a.m. is usually the best window to

68 See www.w4mp.org/library/alt-guides/dean-trench/handling-the-media-what-youve-always-wanted-to-know-about-the-fourth-estate-but-were-afraid-to-ask

send a press release. If the newspaper is published weekly, a press release will need to be sent several days in advance in order for it to be allocated space. Sending a press release the day before publication is too late.

2. Write a good, catchy headline. Just as the reporter will want a headline to catch their audience's attention, the press release needs to grab the eye of the journalist.

3. Write the press release as if it was a story appearing in the paper. It's best to use neutral language and cover all the questions of who, what, where, when and why. Do not be biased as it will just get re-written and may even lessen the chance of the story being used at all.

4. Focus most on the quote. This is the one part of the press release that cannot be edited by the reporter. It's in this section that the political argument can be made. However, the language must remain simple, short and punchy. The quote should read more like a conversation down the pub, rather than a statement in a formal letter.

If the story is attacking something, it will cover:

- What the issue is.
- What the effect of this issue is on the constituency/constituents.
- What the MP thinks should be done about it.

For example: 'The council is wrong to be turning off 40 per cent of the streetlights in our area. This is dangerous and it will put both road users and pedestrians at risk. They should listen to the huge number of concerns raised by local people and switch our lights back on.'

If the story is praising something, it will include:

- The MP welcomes the issue.
- The MP congratulates the people involved.
- The MP wishes them the best for the future .

For example: 'It's great news that local pupils have achieved a record number of A*–C grades in their GCSEs this year. We have excellent schools in this area, with brilliant teachers who work very hard to support pupils to achieve their best. I wish all the pupils the very best as they begin the next chapter of their lives.'

Full examples of press releases for both these stories are included at the end of this book.

1. Add a photo. Most editors now insist that each story they publish online is accompanied by a photo. Photos taken with a smartphone are of sufficient quality to be used online and in print, so you should plan ahead and think through the best image possible to illustrate the story (it's also worth ensuring that your phone always has enough storage space). If you don't supply a photo the reporter will go through their back catalogue of images of your boss and, depending on their fondness of the MP, will pick either a nice photo of them, or an old, grainy picture that does them no favours.

2. Send the text in the email, not as an attachment. The press release needs to be as simple and quick to access as possible for the reporter. Sending it as a document attached in an email is an

extra barrier to it being read. The reporter may also be out of the office with poor 3G signal, so it's best just to include all the text in the main body of the email.

3 Editor's notes: If the press release includes facts or figures, these can be verified in the editor's notes.

4 Contact details: Add your mobile number at the bottom.

5 MP availability: If it's likely that the regional TV or radio news will want to cover the story it is worth stating that 'the MP is available for interviews from 2 p.m. this afternoon', or something to this effect to nudge them towards inviting the MP on to the show.

6 Blind copy: If the press release is going to all local media contacts then the recipients should be added in the 'blind copy' field. If they're added in the normal 'To' field then the first dozen lines of the press release will just be the email addresses of other journalists. You should add yourself to the recipients list in order to receive a copy of the exact email you sent to the reporters (just in case there's any misquoting or misrepresentation).

7 Contact lists: Set up a mailing list of all media contacts on your laptop and mobile phone to a make it easier and quicker to ensure that everyone receives the press release.

HOW TO RESPOND TO MEDIA ENQUIRIES

Journalists will often call you to request a quote from the MP, to set up an interview or request background information on a story they are working on.

If a reporter calls to ask for a quote, you should:

- Ask them to run through the story and explain the angle they would like/expect the MP to take in their comment. Also ask what their deadline is and say you will email back with a quote.

- If you have no background knowledge of the story, call the constituency office to see if any of the staffers there do. If it's about a national issue, you're best calling the party's media team at HQ to ask for their advice.

- Call your MP, or if they're in a meeting or in the House of Commons, text them information about the story, plus a draft quote. Notify the MP when the deadline for getting the quote back to the reporter is.

- When the MP returns the quote with any edits, copy this into a new email and send to the reporter. Write ENDS after the quote so that the reporter knows they have the full text.

If the reporter calls to set up an interview, you should:

- Ask the reporter the same initial questions as with a request for a quote, but also whether the interview will be broadcast live or whether it is a pre-record. Will it be a one-to-one interview, or a discussion? Who will be the interviewer and, if it's a pre-record, how long will the final clip be?

- Send this information to the MP by text or email to ask if they are happy to do the interview.

- If the MP is happy to go ahead, call the reporter back to arrange a suitable time and location. Most TV interviews that take place in Westminster are done either on College Green (a small park to the south of Parliament, which will have Big Ben in the background of the shot) or in the studios at 4 Millbank. If the interview is taking place in the constituency, you will need to provide the address of a suitable location for the interview. This must be a fairly quiet area with a relevant background. Most radio interviews are conducting over the phone. Landlines are preferred but many stations are happy for the MP to use their mobile if this is more convenient.

- Send the MP any background notes for the interview and draft suggested responses to likely questions (often a reporter is happy to let the MP know their questions in advance, so it's worth asking). Make time in the MP's diary for them to practise answers and for you to play the role of the interviewer.

- Whether the interview is taking place in Westminster or the constituency, a staffer should always go along with the MP to check for messy hair, twisted ties and to listen out for any major inaccuracies in the MP's answers. The staffer should also ensure that the camera and microphone is off while the MP is chatting to the reporter.

If the reporter calls to request background information, you should:

- First confirm with the reporter that the conversation is off the record – though not even in off-the-record conversations should you put any words in the mouth of your MP. If you've built up a good relationship with the reporter you will know how much you can trust them not to abuse any off-the-record information.

- Often it will be the case that you don't know everything about the issue the reporter is calling on. Rather than direct the reporter to speak to the MP, office manager or caseworker, it's best for you to find out the information first and then call the reporter back to pass this on. This maintains control of the flow of information going from the MP's office to the reporter – having only one source means there is no discrepancy in information and if there is any misreporting you will know it's the journalist at fault, rather than questioning and suspecting other members of your team. When calling back the reporter, always ask if they want to include a quote or interview with the MP.

Sometimes reporters ask you to help them find case studies for the story. For example, if the story is about a failing GP surgery, they will want to include some personal experiences from constituents who use the practice. In a case such as this, you should:

- Speak to staffers in the local office to see if they can recommend any constituents who would be suitable to be interviewed.
- Contact the constituent to ask if they would be happy to be interviewed. Explain the process involved, how long the filming may take and what they are likely to be asked in the interview.
- If the constituent is happy to do the interview, send an introductory email to both the reporter and constituent. Ask to be copied in to all future emails.

In today's climate of dwindling newspaper sales and huge cuts in reporter numbers, local journalists need their MP just as much – perhaps even more – as the MP needs them. You should try your best to build a positive and trusting relationship with your media contacts to ensure your boss receives regular, positive coverage in the newspaper and local radio.

HOW TO CREATE A WEEKLY MEDIA NOTE

Local journalists are often overstretched and under-supplied on good stories. By introducing a weekly media note you can give your MP the best chance of making it into the local newspaper, or onto the regional radio and TV. This media note will be sent on a Monday morning to all your media contacts with the purpose of alerting them to the some of the MP's key activities in the upcoming fortnight.

Regular notes like this will help you build stronger relationships with local reporters, who will appreciate the effort you're making to be cooperative, proactive and open about the MP's activities. Journalists need to know about events well before they happen. At the same time, a media note gives you an increased ability to control the news coverage. You can state your MP's views and assessments of stories before they happen. You can also earn favours by leaving 'special' events out of the note and then offer these to an individual reporter as an exclusive.

The first step to putting together a media note for the next fortnight begins several weeks before. Working with the staffers in the local office you need to look ahead in the MP's diary and ensure that they have sufficient visits, events and activities planned – both in the constituency and in Westminster – that can be covered by the local media. If there isn't you can then discuss ideas for activities that could be added to the diary; what debates are planned in Parliament that the MP could contribute to? Are there any significant dates that can be used as a peg for an activity? What about working up a successful piece of casework as a story? When there is sufficient content in the diary you can put together the media note for the fortnight ahead.[69]

---

69 Of course, the MP will have many more meetings and engagements planned than those disclosed in the weekly note. These, however, will either be confidential or uninteresting to the media and therefore should not be included

A media note is only a snapshot or teaser of the MP's upcoming activities. You won't therefore want to spend any more than an hour a week putting one together, but they are very useful to do as they help to ensure that the MP's diary is kept full of interesting, relevant and newsworthy activities.

HOW TO WORK WITH REGIONAL TV NEWS

by Emma Hutchinson, regional political correspondent for ITV News

As a regional political correspondent, I am keen to build a good working relationship with MPs and their parliamentary researchers from around the region I cover.

We are keen to get MPs' views and comments and responses into our television reports and of course question MPs on issues relating to their constituencies. It's a two-way street: as a journalist I want to hear from MPs and their constituents, but I believe it's also important for MPs to get their voices onto regional media.

Our main evening news programme is at 6 p.m. and draws a loyal audience. More people watch ITV regional news at 6 p.m. than many 24-hour news channels and national political programmes. And surveys suggest that regional news is one of the most trusted news outlets in the country.

So what kind of stories are we interested in?

At ITV *News* we are essentially interested in telling people's stories and often MPs and their parliamentary researchers come to me with stories from their constituents that are strong issues with a human interest element. Of course, not every constituent will want to talk about their issue on camera, but if they do then a story works better for us on TV if we can get an individual who is prepared to be interviewed and filmed to personalise the issue we are reporting on.

We are also keen to communicate what's going on in Parliament, be it debates on Bills that affect our region or Adjournment debates by local MPs, as well as Questions and select committees. But we want to do so in a way that is both accessible and engaging to our viewers. That's why even if an MP has said their bit in Parliament in a debate or during Question Time or committee we are often keen to get a quick interview on camera to get a shorter, more 'to-the-point' answer.

Though a twenty-second clip may sound awfully short, actually that's the average length of an answer we will put into a report, and in broadcasting terms it's a good length of time. Most of the interviews we will do are pre-recorded, but occasionally we will want to do a live interview, perhaps down the line with a studio presenter.

Communications with regional media

Good communication in this business is essential. I have been a regional news reporter for fifteen years, from the days of pagers and faxes to text messages and Twitter, and as our newsroom has become more digitised, so MPs' communications have also evolved. As a reporter I've found this has made communication between journalist and MP much easier and quicker. In this job many years ago, I would ring an MP's office and perhaps a diligent parliamentary researcher called me back. If not then maybe I heard back hours later, even sometimes days later.

Now much of the communication is done by text or email, with parliamentary researchers and MPs themselves. We often work on a very tight deadline so a quick response, even if it's a 'no, can't do the interview' is better than not hearing back for several hours.

We run an efficient, streamlined operation and if we do an interview with an MP we almost always use it. Occasionally technical gremlins prevent us but we rarely do an interview that we choose to leave out.

So how do MPs and parliamentary researchers build a good relationship with their regional media?

We are keen to hear about what MPs are doing and campaigning on and we are looking for strong, picture-rich stories with a human interest. A press release two days after an event with a photo of an MP might make a weekly newspaper, but it won't make an ITV news bulletin. We want to know about events before they take place and with enough advance notice that we can get there and film it. And, of course, if you want to tell us first then we love an exclusive story.

The reach of regional news is far greater than a local newspaper or a local radio station or indeed many national television programmes. Viewers might not always remember exactly what an MP said, but they will know they have been on TV and note their expression and demeanour. And, of course, when something happens unexpectedly and the call comes from party press officers asking an MP to stand in on *Question Time* or *Newsnight* or the *Today* programme, it's perhaps less nerve-racking if that isn't their first time on TV.

HOW TO WORK WITH LOBBY REPORTERS

While you will want to proactively seek to build relationships with local journalists during your first week in the job, it's usually best to get to know the lobby reporters more naturally through hanging out in the Strangers' Bar, at conference and at the various evening events and receptions you'll attend. There are many hacks in the lobby, and it would take too long to organise a coffee with every one of them.

Lobby reporters are not interested in an MP's day-to-day activities in the same way that local newspapers are. You will therefore only want to contact them when your boss is doing or has done something significant, such as tabling a popular or controversial Private Member's Bill or Westminster Hall debate. MPs who are a shadow minister or a member of a select committee may also reach out to the lobby reporters if they're making an important speech or wanting to launch an attack on the government.

When wanting to contact a lobby reporter, you should:

- First research who is best to contact. Just as local journalists have preferred stories, so too do different lobby reporters working for different national papers. A quick search on Google should find news reports on the issue your MP is wanting to gain coverage of. The journalists who wrote these stories should be the first ones you approach.

- It's best to give the reporter a call (you can do this through the main Houses of Parliament switchboard) and ask for a meeting in Moncrieff's (the canteen next to the office where lobby reporters work). In the meeting you can verbally brief the reporter on the story and why their editor should be interested in covering it.

- Follow this up with a written briefing that you either give the reporter at the meeting or send to them later in an email. This should include a quote and background notes and be written up as if it were the story going into the paper.

Kate McCann is a former parliamentary researcher who is now senior political correspondent at the *Telegraph*. Here she sets out how she believes a parliamentary researchers can effectively engage with her and her lobby colleagues:

The lobby has a reputation for being a bit mysterious – even to those of us working in it. The term is used to describe both the physical

place where political editors and journalists work in Parliament, and also the gaggle of hacks themselves.

It's unusual in that journalists from different papers work in the same room, and a mythical code of lobby rules prevents papers from stealing stories and tips from each other. That said, it's one of only a very few areas of journalism where reporters will share information and work together on stories – so don't be surprised if two hacks offer to take your MP out for lunch together. (It's not a pincer movement – it just saves on the expenses bill!)

Every national newspaper and some regional titles have a political team in the lobby – some TV channels also work in Parliament. Our job as political reporters is to meet MPs and staffers, find out what's going on behind the scenes and build a picture to fill our blank pages every day.

We also attend lobby briefings by the Prime Minister's spokesperson every morning and afternoon to keep on top of what's going on in government. It's a chance to ask questions and get the PM's take via his civil service right-hand man – or woman.

Typically, journalists might call an MP's office to leave an urgent message or to make arrangements for a lunch or coffee. Most hacks will want the mobile number of the member concerned if they don't have it already, and it's up to you and your MP to decide whether you hand it out over the phone or not – some MPs do and others don't.

Despite what some people think about the profession, journalists in Parliament trade on their reputation – it's not in their interest to make MPs look bad unfairly. So a chat 'on background' means anything printed has no names attached – MPs should always make clear whether they are happy to be quoted, or just talk off the record.

On some occasions we have a story in mind already, or events will be unfolding throughout the day and we'll be after a straight comment from an MP, rather than a more relaxed off-the-record conversation which can be saved for a later date.

Often reporters will be on a tight deadline, so it's a good idea to ask how quickly they need a response if the journalist doesn't make it clear. They may need a comment straight away, or be happy to wait a few days for a response regarding the best date for a meeting. If you don't know the answer immediately, don't be afraid to say you don't know and offer to call back. Make sure you always call back.

It's best to be polite and as upfront as you can be, but always stick to your guns. I once called an MP's office about an embarrassing story where the MP himself answered – and pretended to be someone else when he realised it was a hack. I called back twice more and twice he pretended to be someone else before his staffer picked up and pretended she was 'just walking past the office when the phone rang'. It's not worth it – it just makes you look silly.

Try not to assume we're out to trip you up. While some journalists might be looking for a story, often we're calling because we already know the details – we just need a comment. It's also worth trying not to show off. Speaking without knowing how much your MP wants to say or dropping yourself in it by chatting about a risky issue to demonstrate your own wealth of political knowledge is never a good idea. It's always best to run things by your political party's media team if you are not sure how to respond.

It's a good idea to try to build relationships with journalists where you can – so you get a feel for how they operate. This is especially important if your MP has a campaign or issue they want to pursue in Parliament and they're going to want a lot of press attention.

Most newspapers compile their list of stories in the morning at around 10 a.m. That means if your MP is making a speech or tabling something in the House you need to give the journalist a heads up the night before. You can do this by explaining that the information is embargoed until a certain time (when you're happy to see it online, on Twitter or in print); or telling them it's all on background if you're happy to see it in the paper, but don't want your MP's name near the story.

The golden rule is always to remember you're representing your boss – never giving your own take. Even if you think the EU Referendum Bill is a load of rubbish, don't tell that to a journalist or you risk dropping your MP in it. Take your time to come up with decent quotes if your MP is happy to see their name in a story – even if that means offering to email something over to the journalist in fifteen minutes. That way you have enough time to think through what you want to say and avoid feeling pressured into a rushed response on the phone.

Above all else, always be clear what your MP wants to say and where they draw the line. It takes time to get a feel for how your boss speaks in quotes or what they think about certain issues, so don't guess – always ask.

Chapter 8

Engaging and campaigning

WHILE YOU ARE officially employed to only assist an MP with his or her parliamentary business, the truth is that the underlying context of all your work is to support their re-election prospects.

HOW TO RESPOND TO POLICY-LOBBYING CAMPAIGNS

As mentioned earlier, your MP will receive thousands of emails, letters, tweets and Facebook messages, as well as the occasional phone call, from constituents asking for his or her view on a particular policy issue. Responding to these policy-lobbying campaigns will take up a significant proportion of your time.

Whatever the issue, and no matter how often the constituent

makes contact, it is good practice to ensure each and every one of these messages receives a response within a decent amount of time (a week is generally OK for emails and letters, but staffers should try to ensure no tweet or Facebook message takes more than twenty-four hours to be responded to – even if this is just a holding response to ask the constituent to send their query to the MP as an email).

Within this general framework, your boss may want you to prioritise some correspondence above others. Messages that are composed of generic text provided by a charity or pressure group are unlikely to receive anything above a basic level of response (unless the MP is particularly passionate about the cause they're writing on). However, if the correspondence has obviously been written by the constituent themselves, you may bump it up the queue of items needing a response. Former Liberal Democrat Chief Whip (and now Lord) Paul Tyler said that, during his time as an MP, 'Anything that looked like a real message from a real constituent ... got priority.'[70]

While we've seen that some MPs don't believe responding to these campaigns is a good use of their time, most are realising that they present a new opportunity to connect with their electorate. As well as the initial response to the correspondence, MPs can use the contact details the constituent provides to send them further communications, such as a weekly e-newsletter, invites to sign a local petition or updates on a bill that relate to the campaign or cause the constituent first got in touch about. Through these follow-up conversations, the MP is able to build a reputation for listening to constituents, taking up their concerns and keeping in touch.

• • •

70 Robert Rogers and Rhodri Walters, *How Parliament Works*, p. 103

EACH MP WILL have their own way of dealing with correspondence from policy-lobbying campaigns. Some, in order to keep their stationery expenses low, will reply to most by email. Other MPs believe that the physicality of a printed letter, arriving in a House of Commons envelope, exudes gravitas. These MPs will respond to correspondence whether it was received as a letter, email or tweet, by post.

Whatever the MP's preference, the steps below set out how you should approach the task of responding to constituents who write to your MP on policy-related matters.

1. Check the person is a constituent: The technology used by many organisations for their policy-lobbying campaigns should ensure people fill out their full address – though not all do and some only require a name and/or postcode. Sometimes constituents will email policy questions off their own back and fail to provide an address. You can use the electoral register to look up a person's address, however if you can't find the individual, or if is there is more than one constituent with that name, email the constituent to request a full address. This email should explain that parliamentary protocol prohibits MPs from engaging with anyone who is not their constituent, hence why you are getting in touch and not them. If the constituent has contacted the MP over Facebook or Twitter it is best to reply initially, and quickly, to ask them to email with their concern. This helps to verify if the person is a constituent while having the additional bonus of collecting another constituent's email address to add to the MP's e-newsletter mailing list.

2. Draft a response and leave for the MP to check: MPs are allowed to use part of their staffing budget for 'payment to pooled staffing

resources'.[71] This has led to the creation of the Policy Research Unit (for Conservative MPs) and the Parliamentary Research Service (for Labour MPs). These provide 'briefing, research, correspondence and related support' to assist MPs to respond to policy-lobbying campaigns. MPs who pay into these services receive access to a library of template letters which are updated regularly and written in line with the party's frontbench policy. Often they will be checked by the relevant minister or shadow minister's office. You will soon love these template letters as they will save you hundreds of hours' worth of research and writing time each year. The letters produced by the PRU and PRS are usually very high in quality and constituents will be impressed by what they receive.

3 Some campaigns may request your MP to write to a particular secretary of state to pass on the concerns of the constituent. If the MP tends to carry out these requests, a draft of this letter should also be included with the response and left for the MP to check and sign-off.

4 Add the constituent's contact details to the main database: While waiting for the MP to make any edits to the letter you can enter the constituent's contact details into the main database used to track all correspondence. There are a few different pieces of software used by MPs for this purpose, but all allow staffers to attach copies of letters, write comments about the constituent (e.g. 'sends nasty sweary emails – don't send any replies' or 'says letters are a waste of taxpayers' money – always email replies') as well as giving people 'tags'. Tagging constituents allows you to mail merge responses to policy-lobbying campaigns, rather than printing out each response individually. Tagging also makes it easy for the MP, at a later date, to write to or email all the people

71 *Annual Review of the MPs' Scheme of Business Costs and Expenses*, 2015–16, p. 27

who have contacted them on a specific issue to update them on what progress he or she is making on the issue. For example, if the constituent contacted your MP regarding funding for cancer research, you may want to write again a few months later to let them know the MP has secured an Adjournment debate on the issue and will be raising the comments the constituent made in their initial email.

5 Print final copies: When the MP has made any changes and signed off on the letter, print all the responses and leave for them to sign. Some MPs will prefer to use an e-signature to save time.

6 Send: After being signed, you'll be left with a pile of letters to fold and stuff into envelopes.

As well as petitions and lobbying campaigns organised by proffessionals, members of the public are using new digital technology to create 'people-powered' campaigns to apply ever greater pressure on MPs.

In 2013, the *New Statesman* dubbed 38 Degrees 'the real opposition' and ahead of the 2015 general election the site published its own manifesto. The Oxford Internet Institute says the organisation 'capitalises on the Internet's potential to make political action visible to overcome traditional collective action problems. The website's ease of use and the organisation's determination to let its members set the political agenda make this an extremely interesting new tool for political engagement.'[72]

Paul Flynn MP has noticed the impact 38 Degrees has had on the House of Commons, too, stating that 'their campaigns opposing the sell-off of forests and NHS change forced MPs into individual replies. The strength and quality of the opposing arguments

72 See https://home.38degrees.org.uk/about/endorsements

worried coalition MPs. There is evidence that the government's resolve was undermined on both issues.'[73]

Change.org began operating in Britain in 2011. It claims that users of its site achieve around ten victories a week on everything from big national issues, from the campaign to keep women on UK banknotes to the 'No More Page 3' campaign, and the campaign led by Fahma Mohammed that called on Michael Gove, then Secretary of State for Education, to write to all headteachers in the country asking them to inform teachers and parents about Female Genital Mutilation.

Change.org differs from other petition sites in that it is an open, neutral platform (similar to Facebook or Twitter) rather than an organised pressure group. Its approach to engaging MPs is significantly different too. Tom Bage, UK Communications Director at Change.org, says: 'Our approach to email is to not bombard MPs and their parliamentary researchers. Our users' petitions only send emails to the subject of the petition (which in this case would be an MP) at key milestones – such as when the petition receives 500 signatures.'

Bage believes that with 8 million users of Change.org already in the UK, parliamentary researchers should be looking to it to monitor and identify any emerging local issues or campaigns.

> The average amount of signatures it takes for a campaign to win using Change.org is around 200, so the site powers campaigns on lots of the hyperlocal issues which MPs are often really interested in. If there's a school or pub in an MP's constituency that has been threatened with closure, or a roundabout that needs building at the end of a street, then the campaign often starts with a petition on Change.org.

---

73 Paul Flynn MP, *How to Be an MP*, p. 84

Importantly, MPs are able to interact with users of Change.org directly through the site by using the 'Decision Maker' tool. According to Bage, 'This has already been successfully used by Nick Clegg MP, Matthew Hancock MP and Stella Creasy MP, and is something all parliamentary researchers should be signing their boss up for as soon as possible.'

• • •

PETITIONS HAVE FOR many years been the most popular form of political participation in Western democracies. Today, their online versions on platforms like Change.org and 38 Degrees, and the policy-lobbying campaigns led by charities and pressure groups, are growing enormously, and will continue to do so over the next few years. Even HM Government have their own e-petition website, which promises that petitions that collect over 100,000 signatures could be debated in the House of Commons (though very few that reach this mark receive attention), and those that collect 10,000 will receive a government response. (Following the relaunch of the site in July 2015 the first petition to reach both these marks called for MPs 'To debate a vote of no confidence in Health Secretary the Right Hon. Jeremy Hunt').

You need to be skilled at responding to policy-lobbying campaigns in a thorough and timely manner. You should also be using sites like Change.org and 38 Degrees to look ahead to developing issues, and encouraging your MP to engage with them where appropriate, either directly by signing a petition or by taking an action in the House of Commons on behalf of their constituents who have.

Owing to the growing number of campaigns and campaigners, if you're not aware and on top of all this incoming correspondence you risk becoming swamped. Those MPs and parliamentary researchers who embrace these new forms of political participation can successfully use them as a first step to developing a deeper level of engagement with their electorate.

HOW TO BUILD A LARGE DATABASE AND THEN USE IT EFFECTIVELY

Building a good mailing list is fundamental to creating a successful digital strategy. This needs to be comprised of both a high quantity of subscribers, as well as sufficient quality of data about the people that are on it. An MP is unlikely to win many new votes by only sending their e-newsletters to party members. Equally, it's difficult to know how effective an e-newsletter is if the only information you have about the audience is their email addresses; you want their name and postcode so that they can be verified as constituents and cross-referenced with your main voter identification database. You should, therefore, invest time and energy into making sure there are numerous ways of gathering constituents' data and adding them to the MP's mailing list.

An easy way of building a mailing list is, as mentioned in 'How to respond to policy-lobbying campaigns', to opt constituents into it by default when they first contact the MP on any casework or policy matter. All major online retailers add their customers to their mailing lists by default, so this is a fairly standard practice and it doesn't annoy many people; providing of course they're given a simple way of unsubscribing should they wish to receive no further emails.

There are strict guidelines to prevent MPs from using data they obtain from constituents through parliamentary duties (such as through casework or a policy-lobbying campaign) for political purposes (for example, sending them a 'vote for me' email the day before a general election). For an e-newsletter to adhere to these rules, it must only focus on information and news about the MP's parliamentary activities, such as speeches made in the Commons, visits to schools and businesses and other relevant local news.[74] In addition, it must not include any overtly political language, logos, rosettes or images associated with the party.

You will want to add a big 'sign-up' button in a prominent position on your MP's website homepage. Analytic tools such as Google Analytics can be used to test a) the best position for this button to be on the screen and b) the most effective form of text. Put both of these insights together to find the most successful combination for encouraging people to submit their details.

The websites for most of the political parties go further than this. In June 2015, visitors to the sites of the Conservatives, Labour, Liberal Democrats and the Green Party were all met first by a 'splash' page which had the primary purpose of gathering as many people's contact details as possible.

Adding constituents to the mailing list by default, and having effective sign-ups like a splash page are two constant devices you can use to build the number of subscribers to your boss's mailing list. But, to complement these, you should also devise some 'pop-up' initiatives, such as surveys, petitions and polls.

Any paper survey or petition that your MP and local volunteers are delivering through constituents' doors, such as 'Tell me your views on local transport' or 'Save our ambulance station. Sign your name here' should be doubled-up and posted online too. As all the text is already written, this is a very quick process. Many website platforms, such as NationBuilder and WordPress, have survey and petition features. However, a simple one can quickly be designed through Google Drive that will do the job just as well.

As well as doubling-up surveys and petitions, the MP could conduct regular polls of constituents. These can ask them to identify

---

74 There are of course ways around this with clever use of language. For example, a door-to-door canvassing session can be rebranded as a 'street surgery'

their top three policy priorities for the year ahead or ask a yes/no question about an issue in their local area ('SNAP POLL: Are you happy with our levels of streetlighting? Yes or No?'). Taken further, an MP can use these same digital tools to ask their constituents to help them to write a speech. In 2015, Andy Sawford delivered a speech in the House of Commons on the subject of 'Corby's fire service', which was composed of comments made by about 200 constituents; the first of its kind. This was done by placing a short blog on Sawford's website that set out the intention to use as many comments made by constituents as possible. This was then promoted on social media and later in his weekly e-newsletter.

As with Andy Sawford's crowd-sourced fire service speech, all surveys should be promoted through the MP's social media channels, as well as in future e-newsletters. You can also issue a press release on the launch of the survey to try to get some local coverage, and if there's room in the budget, set up adverts on Facebook, Twitter and Google to target specific areas or demographics within the constituency.

It is important that the MP responds to everyone who takes part in one of these surveys, petitions or polls to thank them for their time and for sharing their views. This is best done by email and should also explain to the constituent what the MP is going to do with the information they've gathered, for example by raising the issue in the House of Commons during Prime Minister's Questions. If constituents are not thanked and made to feel appreciated in this way, they are far less likely to bother taking part in any further positive engagement with the MP. If, however, they do feel that their time has been well spent, they are more likely to become further engaged with the MP by tweeting or sharing posts on social media or, over time perhaps, volunteering to take part in future campaigns.

Why are surveys, petitions and polls effective? Because people want the opportunity to express themselves and feel like their voice is heard. Done well, these devices provide a simple way for constituents to do this, while allowing you to collect data and information on hundreds, possibly thousands of people, all of whom can be sent further e-newsletters and updates containing positive information about their MP.

As well as these 'pop up' initiatives, an MP should also use their social media channels to occasionally nudge their followers to sign up to his or her e-newsletter. If these messages are accompanied with an engaging image, such as featuring a positive quote about the e-newsletter from another constituent, a nice picture of the MP or a catchy teaser of the next mail out, they will successfully encourage a handful of people each time to add themselves to the mailing list.

Finally, every e-newsletter or thank-you email to those who take part in a survey should always include an 'ask'. This will be to prompt the constituent to take some form of action. For example, to forward the email on to friends and family, or to share a post that the MP has put on their Twitter or Facebook page.

If all of these initiatives are carried out successfully, an MP can expect to collect between fifty and 100 new subscribers to their mailing list each week. The underlying strategy of all of this is:

1. By focusing on non-political issues, the MP is projecting themselves as a dedicated, hard-working local champion.

2. Having a constituent take a small action like filling out a survey or sharing something on Facebook can lead to them taking bigger actions in the future, such as volunteering during the general election campaign by taking part in a phone bank or delivering leaflets.

A constituent is only likely to go on this online journey from stranger to supporter if the content of e-newsletters, surveys and the

MP's social media channels are of a high and engaging standard. E-newsletters should, therefore, look to incorporate lots of images and graphics and as little text as possible. If something needs a long explanation, an MP can post this on their Facebook page or website and link to it in the e-newsletter.

HOW TO CREATE A SUCCESSFUL E-NEWSLETTER

The layout of the e-newsletter must also be easy for the reader to follow. More and more people are now using their mobile or tablet device for the majority of their online reading. By 2018, the number of smartphone owners in the UK is expected to reach 46 million, so an e-newsletter should be designed in a format that is optimised for mobile devices. Additionally, an e-newsletter should be broken down into clearly labelled sections to help the reader find the content they're most interested in. These sections could include:

- Picture of the week: the best image of the MP – ideally an action shot. This section could also be video of the week.

- Facebook post of the week: a screengrab of a post from Facebook is an eye-catching way of displaying the MP's post and has the added bonus of promoting their Facebook page.

- Top 5: a list of the MP's five most important activities of the week

- Debates in Parliament: a short summary of some of the key debates and votes in the House of Commons that week.

- 'Community noticeboard': a space where constituents can ask

> the MP to post information about local events, such as charity fundraisers and village fairs.

Most voters will have never before been given the option of receiving such regular feedback from their MP, so an e-newsletter can be a refreshing and humanising approach. It is also a chance for the MP to illustrate, or prove, how busy they are and to demonstrate their relevance to the day-to-day lives of their electorate, such as by giving updates on what he or she is doing to sort out potholes across the area, or to improve reliability of local bus services.

Data from a number of MPs shows that e-newsletters are popular and, on average, achieve open rates well over 20 per cent, with some MPs averaging over 35 per cent. This means that a good e-newsletter is likely to achieve 1,000–2,000 opens. Though this may seem small, as one parliamentary researcher who produces a very successful e-newsletter on behalf of their MP explains:

> At most, 45,000 people will vote at a general election in our constituency, so to have a readership of 2,500 people each week means that my boss has an audience concentration for his e-newsletter of 5.5 per cent. This is far higher than any national newspaper in the area and pretty good compared to evening regional news programmes. More importantly, though, we're sharing unfiltered content, direct from the MP to the voter. We also get to collect lots of further data that tells us who clicks on which links and what issues most interest the readers. We can then use all this new information to help design future campaigns and target people who we might be able to turn into volunteers at the election, and even party members.

You can use the following list to assess the success of your e-newsletter and identify areas for improvement that will drive up open rates and the number of people completing your 'ask'.

- Subject line: this can have a huge impact over how many people open the email. Some MPs prefer consistency, such as Stella Creasy MP who uses 'Working for Walthamstow Newsletter' as the subject for each edition. Others will tailor each week's subject line to pick out a key message to draw the recipient into pressing the 'open' button.

- Time and day: it's much more effective to send an e-newsletter at 3 p.m. on a Friday afternoon than at 10 p.m. on a Sunday evening. Both NationBuilder and MailChimp allow users to schedule e-newsletters to be sent at a specific time.

- What is the 'ask'? Each newsletter should ask the reader to take an action. This could be to sign a petition, take part in a survey or share a post on Facebook. Whatever the ask is, it needs to be clearly written and physically stand out by being placed in a button or in bold font (you may even want to use a flashing GIF image to really make the ask stand out).

- Test, test and test again: before pressing the 'send' button, press the 'test' one several times to check that all the pictures look OK, all the links work as they should and all the text is formatted correctly to fit both mobile and laptop screens.

- Evaluate performance: before sending the next e-newsletter, check how the last one performed. Was the email header more or less successful than previous editions at getting people to open it? Did lots of people carry out the 'ask'? Did one link to the MP's website work better than all the rest? How many people unsubscribed? The analytics tools on NationBuilder and MailChimp will allow you to answer these questions, as well as giving you data on what devices people read the email on and what time of day they opened it. You should regularly evaluate this information to see what adjustments can be made to your e-newsletter to increase its readership and levels of engagement.

- Look around for new ideas: subscribe to other MPs' newsletters, and those of politicians in other countries, digital agencies and innovative businesses for inspiration.

As people increasingly consume news and find information over the internet, e-newsletters have the potential to become one of the primary sources of local knowledge for many constituents. Rather than traditionally having their work communicated via the local newspaper, MPs can now speak direct to thousands of constituents and monitor with precision who is reading what, who is taking actions on their behalf and, ultimately, who is mostly likely to support them at the next election.

HOW TO LISTEN ONLINE

For an MP to earn the attention of their local online community, they first need to demonstrate that they are genuinely engaged with the area.

The internet was first about creating easy and cheap ways to eradicate geography and connect people over vast distances. Today, much of the internet is about connecting people with place – where they live, where they work, where they are at that very minute. You should use digital technology first to 'listen-in' and monitor local news and conversations voters are having with each other. Putting it bluntly, your job is to follow the local electorate wherever they go online.

The digital spaces that people use to find news about their local area, discuss issues with neighbours in the community and pressure political representatives from vary enormously. Take the Streatham parliamentary constituency for example. Located in a vibrant part of south-west London, it covers Brixton Hill, Clapham Common, St Leonard's, Streatham Hill, Streatham South, Streatham Wells, Thornton and Tulse Hill. It is served by many different forms of traditional, new and social media. There is the *Evening Standard*, which is a free, London-wide evening newspaper. The *Standard* will cover any major events that happen in the area. Then there is the *South London Press* and the *Streatham Guardian* and *Wandsworth Guardian* (which covers part of Clapham Common), which will all be reporting daily on news from the area. The constituency has many online forums or hyperlocal blogs such as Urban75, the Brixton Blog (which also prints 10,000 copies of the 'free, monthly community newspaper', the *Brixton Bugle*), BrixtonBuzz, the Herne Hill Forum (which covers parts of Tulse Hill) and the Streatham Common Forum, as well as several groups on the Streetlife and Mumsnet networks, each of which contain several hundred members. Indeed, a member of the Streatham Mumsnet group says, 'I strongly believe we have a bigger influence on local politicians that any traditional news outlet in this area.' Further diversity is then provided by numerous conversations taking place about the area on Facebook, Instagram and Twitter, as well as petitions set up on Change.org, 38 Degrees or an individual person's blog.

An MP's office needs to be monitoring as many of these conversations as possible in order to identify any emerging issues or concerns. Where necessary, you should advise your MP to enter the conversations and work to resolve the issues. As Callum Hood demonstrates in 'How to get your boss re-elected', MPs have 'an authority to pick up local issues and make changes in their area that no one else does'.

- Google news searches can be narrowed down to fetch results from either news sites or blogs. A search for the name of an area, e.g. 'Streatham' will produce results from any traditional news service, such as the *Evening Standard* and *Streatham Guardian* reporting on the area, as well as any hyperlocal news sites like the Brixton Blog.

- Visit these sites and subscribe to their RSS feeds or e-newsletter. You can use RSS readers, such as 'The Old Reader', Feedly or Flipboard, to collate all their RSS feeds into one single channel (in a similar way that a Facebook news feed collates all the latest posts from your friends). Using RSS feeds in this way means that rather than going to each of these different news sites and hyperlocal blogs one-by-one, you can just visit one web page which will show you all the latest updates from relevant sources in the constituency. Other forums such as Streetlife will offer a daily newsletter that will include a feed of all the latest conversations to have started on their platform about the area in the last twenty-four hours. You will want to be subscribed to this. Often constituents will initiate conversations such as: 'No household bins have been emptied on my road for the last three weeks. Same anywhere else?' If that conversation receives lots of contributions, it means it's an issue your MP needs to act on. Alert your MP and constituency office to this and work collaboratively to decide the best way for the MP to intervene. In this example of bins not being collected:

    - The MP could call or write an urgent letter to the local council and arrange to meet with local residents to see what impact the build-up of all this waste is having.

    - The MP should post a comment in the forum's thread to say something along the lines of 'I've read your comments, I have raised this problem with the council and I'm told the council will arrange for bins to be collected tomorrow. I'll be visiting this afternoon to speak to local residents and see the impact this is having on your street.' Most constituents will be impressed that their MP is listening to their concerns and acting on them in such a fast and proactive manner.

- Increasingly, communities are setting up petitions online through platforms like Change.org. In Brixton, a petition to 'Halt the evictions of Brixton and Herne Hill's beloved businesses' from their positions under railway arches has collected 25,000 signatures (and was initiated by the Brixton Blog). Politicians can respond positively to these petitions. One set up by residents in Streatham Hill, calling on Transport for London to make the A23 road safer (the road runs right through the high street), has attracted the attention of lots of local politicians (councillors, the MP and MEP), who are now all working with the residents who set up the online petition to campaign for action.

- You need to follow all local professional and community-led news services on Facebook and Twitter. Often information will appear on social media before being posted on their website. As these sites are often run by well-respected, well-liked members of the community, it is useful for the MP to occasionally retweet or share a post of theirs to show they're 'in touch' with the area and passionate about local issues.

- You will also want to monitor local 'influencers' – residents of the local community who have a powerful voice. They may be shop owners, people who run small charities, business managers or simply an individual who is passionate about their local area. These can be found by looking to see who local reporters or hyperlocal bloggers follow. They're likely to have a big following on social media, so it's useful to know what they're saying, and to help your MP to engage with them. By following these people on social media, you will pick up on any local hashtags that might be trending and getting a lot of people talking. In the case of the petition to improve safety along the A23 road in Streatham, every time there is an accident along the road Twitter fills with local residents using the hashtag #A23safety to highlight the issue. MPs who do engage in local issues online will often find they receive lots of positive comments, retweets and shares. Some MPs may still consider social media to be a poor return on their time. Actually, the bigger risk posed by social media is being absent from the conservation.

- Following all these different people, organisation and hashtags can be tricky. Invest some time in organising them all into Twitter lists, and then use either Hootsuite or TweetDeck to bring all these lists together into one space. This means that, on one screen, you can see:

    - A list of local reporters and people.
    - A stream of their MP's tweets.
    - A stream of tweets about their MP.
    - A stream of people from the Westminster Village (other MPs, lobby reporters).
    - A stream of keywords from the constituency e.g. 'Streatham' and 'Brixton'.
    - A stream of any key hashtags e.g. '#A23safety'.

By using a combination of RSS feeds, newsletter subscriptions and following key local organisations, people and hashtags on social media, you will pick up on news and issues quickly and develop a strong sense of local opinion.

HOW TO ENGAGE ONLINE

Next, you to need to support you MP to create a genuine dialogue online with their electorate. As Deborah Mattinson, Gordon Brown's chief pollster, says in her book *Talking to a Brick Wall*, 'Listening is crucial, but is only half the story. An honest conversation between politicians and voter is needed too.'[75] An MP's social media, website and e-newsletter are vital tools towards creating this 'honest conversation'. Rather than being restricted to soundbite comments on the radio or TV, or just a few sentences in the newspaper, new digital communications platforms allow for consistent, detailed and genuine conversations to take place between the elector and the elected. Continuing with the Streatham constituency, the local MP Chuka Umunna won many plaudits in the area when he directed a number of tweets at Southern Rail to complain about their 'consistently late' services and called for some of the company's franchises to be taken over by Transport for London.[76]

An MP should no longer simply proclaim to be working on solving a problem, such as poor train services, when they can use digital communications to tell the story as they take each step from experiencing the problem themselves, to contacting the organisation responsible (they can post an image of their letter), and raising the issue in the House of Commons. It's by telling stories like this, with engaging images, videos and text, that an MP is able to demonstrate the value of the work they do.

In 2010, Deborah Mattinson ran a series of focus groups that asked members of the public why they felt politics was failing to engage more of the population, and what they thought

---

75 Deborah Mattinson, *Talking to a Brick Wall* (London: Biteback Publishing, 2011), p. 293

76 See www.standard.co.uk/news/transport/chuka-umunna-in-twitter-row-with-rail-bosses-over-consistently-late-trains-9977307.html

politicians could do to rebuild trust. Mattinson found there to be a 'dysfunctional relationship' containing a huge gap between the Westminster Village and everyone else. She says:

> The Westminster Village has changed. It has become more rarified, increasingly made up of politicians and journalists who have a very single-minded focus on the political process. But while the Westminster Village has looked in on itself, the public want more outward-looking MPs. No longer content for them to be the remote and one-dimensional figure that typified Mrs Thatcher back in the 1980s, voters now demand to see politicians in the round: to know about their backgrounds, their families, their hobbies, their homes – to get to know them as people.[77]

Social media, e-newsletters and websites are the channels through which MPs can show themselves in the round. Alongside their professional work, they can show they have a family, support football teams, play musical instruments, have hobbies and are, beneath the suit, a real person.

Steve Hatch, Facebook's UK & Ireland director, explains the integral role Facebook now plays in British politics, and how it was used by some leading politicians during the 2015 general election:

Members of Parliament right across the United Kingdom are turning to Facebook to get their messages out and connect directly with the people who elect them. In fact, during the run-up to the general election, nearly all candidates running a close race turned to Facebook to encourage people to vote. On Facebook, we saw more than 78 million interactions from 12 million people related directly to the election in the run-up to 7 May. These people were talking about the

---

77 Deborah Mattinson, *Talking to a Brick Wall*, p. 287

candidates and the issues that matter most to them. A week before election day, the most-discussed topic on Facebook switched from health to the economy. Throughout the campaign, the most-discussed party leader was David Cameron.

The reason for this trend is clear. Studies show that using Facebook effectively can have a massive impact on a campaign, whether it's building trust with people or encouraging people to vote. In 2012, a *Nature* magazine study examining the 2010 mid-term elections in the United States showed that when people see that their friends have voted, they themselves are inspired to vote – on a scale that influenced more than 342,000 people to go to the polls. As Teddy Goff, Digital Director for 'Obama for America', famously said, 'People don't trust campaigns ... Who do they trust? Their friends.'

Building trust with people on Facebook comes in a variety of guises and is possible on an incredible scale. Politicians turn to their status updates to share with people their reactions to issues as they unfold, or their reason for voting 'yes' or 'no'. What's most compelling about these kinds of updates on Facebook is that even though the text tends to be quite long, the performance of these posts does extraordinarily well. This is a phenomenon that is quite unique to the space of politics and governance. Whereas often in social media the goal is to limit the amount of text you're using, in politics people actually want to get inside the heads of the people who are representing them politically: to think and to observe and to reflect and to notice the ways that their political representatives are thinking, observing, reflecting and noticing.

Members of Parliament globally are also becoming extremely adept at adopting the latest technology available to them to connect with people via Facebook. Question-and-answer sessions are increasingly popular on Facebook as they allow politicians to take questions directly from people, at a scale that wouldn't be possible in person. Nicola Sturgeon mastered this art during the lead-up to the Scottish Referendum and later the UK general election, going

so far as to host a Facebook Q&A on the day of the election itself. Her Q&As alone have been known to double her fan count on her Facebook page. MPs used Facebook video updates to share with constituents the work they were doing in their geographic region; or to update people on their travels.

Whether a politician is tucked away in a corner office in the European Parliament overlooking Place Luxembourg, or is a newly appointed minister arriving on day one to a freshly formed Cabinet, Facebook is the place where leaders and decision-makers are connecting directly to people, no matter where they live or what languages they speak.

These figures from Facebook are quite incredible, and MPs ignore them at their peril. On average, 18,461 people in each constituency interacted 6.5 times with politics through Facebook ahead of the general election. The question is, then, how do you instigate interaction with an MP's Facebook page? As Hatch says, posts that are relatively long achieve a high level of engagements. On 29 June 2015, Prime Minister David Cameron posted text that was over 1,000 words long on his Facebook account outlining his response to the beach attack by terrorists in Tunisia.[78] This was liked, shared and commented on thousands of times as concerned members of the public wanted to engage in the issue.

Native videos are becoming increasing popular too. These are videos that are uploaded to or created on Facebook or Twitter and played in-feed, rather than being a link taking the audience to the video hosted elsewhere (such as YouTube). By the end of 2014, more than 3 billion video views were taking place each day on Facebook (with more than 2 billion photos now shared daily on Facebook, Instagram, Facebook Messenger and

---

78 https://www.facebook.com/DavidCameronOfficial/posts/1011883455502639

WhatsApp). Staffers can record videos of the MP on their smartphones while out campaigning or taking part in local events or in the parliamentary office for them to provide a brief explanation of their views on an important vote in the Commons. These videos should tease an MP's followers into watching with good introductory text, and include an ask for viewers to like and share the video with their friends.

You should ensure your MP's Facebook page is updated at least once a day. This should be a mixture of text, video, photos and images.[79] For this content to achieve high levels of engagement, it must be tailored to the audience and to the style of Facebook. Simply copying the same text from Twitter (including usernames and hashtags) won't engage the audience as effectively.

Facebook also has an analytics system to allow you to monitor the reach of each post and 'learn about your target audience so you can create more relevant content for them'.[80] This includes:

- Demographic information about your target audience, including trends about age and gender, relationship status, and job roles.

- Lifestyle and interest information about your target audience.

You can use this data to set up tailored advertisements on Facebook to promote the surveys, campaigns and initiatives that the MP is running to certain demographics (for example, adverts for a transport survey can be targeted at people identified as being a commuter, car owner or rail passenger). You may also want to run ongoing adverts for the MP's Facebook page that encourage more

79 Infographics provide effective ways of getting key messages out. Rather than a quote or statement simply being posted as text, a staffer can turn it into a colourful image. Tools like infogr.am are free and easy to use for these purposes, though Adobe design software can be purchased through expenses

80 See www.facebook.com/help/528690393907960?sr=8&query=insights&sid=18S7f0Z4HGvL3M067

people to 'like' it (meaning the MP's posts will start appearing on more people's news feeds).

When this targeting functionality is used effectively, Facebook has the power to be a key weapon in marginal constituencies. In an article for the *Daily Telegraph* headlined 'The secrets of the Tory war room', Tim Ross explains how the Conservatives used audience data on Facebook as part of their armoury to target key voters in the build-up to the general election:[81]

> Using data from Facebook ... the Tories were able to identify the key concerns of small groups of undecided voters, for example women in their forties who were concerned about schools and GP opening hours, in specific districts of key marginal seats. During the final days of the election campaign, these voters were targeted repeatedly, on the phone, via websites and in person on the doorstep.

An MP's website should be thought of as being the home for all their digital communication, though it is itself one of their least active channels. Whereas Twitter and Facebook may be updated daily, an MP may only post on their blog once a week. As social media increasingly becomes the channel through which an MP shares news of their work, their websites, more and more, are about collecting data on constituents.

The platform that most ably demonstrate this is NationBuilder. It was used by the Conservatives, Labour, Liberal Democrats and UKIP, both nationally and at candidate level, before, during and after the general election. It combines three elements that are core to an MP's digital strategy:

1. A website that hoovers up data on constituents.

---

81 See www.telegraph.co.uk/news/politics/11609570/Secrets-of-the-Tories-election-war-room.html

2 A database that stores this information and allows for segmentation and tagging.

3 An email system that allows thousands of messages to be sent, and collects data on open rates and click-throughs.

Toni Cowan-Brown, vice-president of European business development to NationBuilder, says:

> Over the last three years, MPs have used NationBuilder to execute a variety of tasks including email newsletters, community surveys, event RSVPs, and volunteer management. The software is built to guide supporters along a ladder of engagement. It starts at the lowest level with passive actions, like Facebook comments or Twitter follows, and moves up to the most proactive ones: becoming a regular volunteer, hosting an event, or donating.

Guiding constituents along a 'ladder of engagement' is what your digital strategy should be all about.

Done well, listening to the local community, picking up on issues and then using the power of an MP's profile to (successfully) campaign on them has the ability to draw constituents into a deeper, more honest relationship. This, in turn, demonstrates an MP to be not just someone who sits shouting in the Commons during PMQs, but a normal person who is passionate about the area and committed to their role as a servant to their constituents.

HOW TO RUN A PHONE BANK

Phone banks are particularly useful for contacting hard-to-reach voters such as those who live in high-rise flats in city centres or remote villages in rural areas. For example, throughout the

2015 general election campaign, all the major political parties were engaged in extensive phone-bank operations, with hundreds of thousands of calls made to targeted segments of the electorate.

Phone banks can be easy to organise and each party will allow MPs and staffers to use desk phones at their London headquarters to run them. You will, however, probably find it much easier to conduct phone-bank sessions in the office or even a quiet corner of one of Parliament's canteens while you wait for that evening's votes. All you need for a phone bank is a script, a call sheet, a pen and a mobile phone.

Below are a few things to consider when organising a phone bank:

1 People are more likely to volunteer if the MP will be present, so pick a date and time that they're free. If you're using landlines at Party HQ, these will need to be booked in advance.

2 Send a message to people who have previously indicated they would help out in a phone bank. If the phone bank is being held at Party HQ for a non-London MP, then the number of possible volunteers will be very small and a staffer can do this simply by text message. If, however, the phone bank is taking place in the constituency, a mass email from the MP to all party members and volunteers is probably the most time-efficient way of asking for help.

3 Before printing call sheets off the central database, liaise with the MP about which area of the constituency the phone bank should target, and what information the script should seek to elicit from people.

4 Make things as easy as possible for volunteers and ensure

they don't at any time feel that their time is being wasted. The organiser should be at the venue early and have all the call sheets and scripts printed out, along with lots of spare pens, ready for the volunteers as they arrive.

5 Prior to making calls, give the volunteers a quick briefing on the aim of the phone bank, such as demographics of the area they're calling, what questions they're asking, why they're asking them and what the MP does with this data.

6 Check regularly that the volunteers are OK with the task and listen out for any difficulties anyone may be having with their call.

7 It's always nice to stop the phone bank a few minutes early and thank everyone for their time by offering to buy them a drink down the local pub, or have pizza or curry delivered to the venue.

8 The next day, ensure that all the data collected during the phone bank is entered into the central database. If any follow-up letters are required, these should be prioritised and sent out in the next forty-eight hours.

9 Securely dispose of all papers from the phone bank.

Your phone bank will consist of two parts. The first – and most important – is the voter identification aspect of the conversation. Here you're seeking to identify electors into one of six general categories:[82]

82 First-time voters obviously do not fit into these categories, but the same theory applies in that the caller will seek to find out which party they are thinking of voting for

1. They are supporters of the party and will vote for the MP/ candidate at the next general election.

2. They have voted for the party in the past, but are unlikely to do so at the next general election.

3. They haven't voted for the party in the past, but are likely to do so at the next general election.

4. They haven't yet made up their mind as to who they might vote for.

5. They haven't voted for the party in the past, and never will vote for the party in the future.

6. They don't vote.

You will want to store this information in a central database that will be used by both the national party and your MP to target the voter with relevant follow-up information. For example, you need to send different information and statements about your MP to a voter placed into category two compared to voters placed in category three. Scrap anyone you put into category five or six as any effort you put into them will be wasted – you're not going to win them round to your cause.

Prior to the 2015 general election, both the Conservatives and Labour used this system to identify former voters who were thinking of switching to the UK Independence Party and directed tailored letters and leaflets to them about the EU referendum (from the Conservatives) and a new, tougher stance on immigration (from Labour).

Individual MPs can take similar follow-up actions; if the caller makes a note of any specific concerns the constituent may have, such as on fracking or animal welfare, a parliamentary researcher can ensure they receive a letter over the next few days from whichever MP is addressing these issues. This can be followed up further with a knock on the door during a future canvassing session.[83] Wally Clinton, who has specialised in using phone banks in presidential campaigns in the US over the last forty years, says, 'The follow-up is probably more important than the actual phone call. One telephone call will not persuade a voter to vote for us. It's the repetition of contacts.'[84]

The second element of a phone bank can be a survey that asks constituents a few short questions about a specific policy or issue. The theme of these questions should be fairly universal, so that whoever picks up the phone will have some view on it – health services, road conditions, crime, jobs and employment are all good ones. The reasons for including some survey questions in the phone-bank script is that, firstly, people like to feel their MP is interested in their opinions. Second, some people are suspicious of telling a stranger over the phone who they may vote for – especially a long way out from an election – so using survey questions at least ensures some data is gathered from the call. Sometimes this conversation can open the voter up to hinting towards their political allegiance. Third, the MP and their team can use the information to identify any developing problems or concerns and take appropriate action.

Phone banks are organised so that all calls are made to a similar postcode. A script asking questions on health issues may collect a number of responses raising similar concerns about the local GP practice. The MP will use this information to seek a meeting with the practice, put the concerns of their constituents to the doctors and talk through any positive steps that both sides can take

83 If an elector is categorised as being a strong supporter of another party, or is a non-voter, then they will be struck off the database and no further contact will be made with them

84 See www.npr.org/2012/07/31/157678602/phone-banks-a-staple-of-campaigning-since-1968

to resolve the situation. If necessary the MP can also look to use the House of Commons to raise the issue with the Health Secretary to seek his or her view, and maybe a meeting to discuss the issue further if necessary. Following this, the MP will write back to all those constituents spoken to during the phone bank and let them know what he or she has done as a result of their feedback.

As well as asking the right questions, the tone of the volunteers needs to be right in order to gather the necessary data. The following extract from a page on MyBarackObama.com summarises the approach Barack Obama wanted his phone-bank volunteers to take:

Smile! This is the most basic rule of voter contact. If you sound like you are enjoying yourself, people will be more interested in engaging in conversation with you and discussing what issues are important to them. Even on the phone, people can tell if you are smiling!

Stay positive! As a volunteer, you're here to excite voters about the President's agenda and the work Organizing for America is doing – not to weigh them down with complaints about the opposition or their viewpoints. Comparisons are good, but keep a positive focus on the President's goals.

Don't pretend to be a policy expert. It's likely that someone will ask you a question to which you do not know the answer. That's okay. You should never be afraid to admit you do not know the details of one of the President's policies. If you aren't sure, say just that. You can point them to WhiteHouse.gov or BarackObama.com for more information on the particular issue.

Follow the script, but speak from the heart. You will have a script to help you engage voters. But think of it as a guide. You will always be more effective if you can clearly and concisely explain what inspired you to work with Organizing for America.[85]

---

85 See https://my.barackobama.com/page/content/phonebankguide

HOW TO FUNDRAISE

Depending on the size of their majority, MPs will want to raise between £30,000 and £50,000 to fight their re-election campaign. Traditionally, the main proportion of an election campaign fund would come from local party membership, but, as fewer and fewer people are paid-up members of political parties, MPs will need to plan a number of fundraising activities to build their war chest.

The type of fundraiser that will absorb the most energy and inflict the most stress on you are the formal, three-course dinners that take place at a hotel somewhere inside the Westminster Village. Guests will pay around £100 a head to attend, so the pressure is on to ensure everything goes well.

While ticket prices are steep, the venue will pocket two-thirds of the amount to cover the costs of the food, alcohol and staff. This means MPs will incorporate an auction into the evening, which, they hope, will be the real money-spinner. Signed sports shirts, holidays, trips to football matches, a bottle of wine signed by the leader of the party, golf tours and official copies of significant government Bills are some of the likely lots the auction will include. It'll be your job to arrange and collect these. Each item individually can raise anywhere between £50 and £5,000.

Here's how to organise a formal fundraiser with an auction:

- Pick a venue: Call a few hotels around Westminster to ask for quotes. You will probably be looking for a room that can hold 150 people, and will be able to provide a three-course meal with wine.

- Arrange a date: If you are having a special guest auctioneer or speaker you will need to check available dates with them. You also want a date when Westminster is at its busiest – the weeks around the Budget and Autumn Statement are the prime times.

- Set up an email account: Because this is a political event, not a parliamentary one, you are unable to use your work email for any of its organisation.

- Target tables, not individual seats: Rather than selling lots of individual tickets, it's best to try to sell tables (which usually have ten places) to organisations, who will then invite their contacts and clients to join them.

- Find the auction items: Work with the MP to identify possible auction prizes. The MP may, for example, have links with a football team or someone who owns a holiday company that may be able to donate an item. For items such as bottles of wine or whisky signed by the leader of the party, these can be arranged by calling their private office.

- Ensure the seating plan is correct: The people who are likely to spend the most money at the auction are usually given the better places at the dining tables in the middle of the room.

- Get to the venue early: You will want time to arrange the auction items and speak with the maître d' about how you want the timings of the evening to take place. For example, you may want the auction to begin after people have finished their main course, but before the dessert is served.

MPs will also arrange fundraising events in the constituency, such as dinners, BBQs, Race Nights (where people bet on videos of old horse races), casino nights or talks by a senior party figure or celebrity. Ticket sales from these events (which can be sold through PayPal, Billetto or Eventbrite), complemented by a raffle, should bring in a couple of thousand pounds.

Political parties are quickly increasing the amount of work they put into seeking smaller donations online from members of the public. In an article published in June 2015 titled 'The story of the Tory stealth operation that outwitted Labour last month', Mark Wallace, *ConservativeHome*'s executive director, says, 'Fundraising online, via small donations from large numbers of people, grew dramatically during the course of the campaign, and is viewed by Conservative fundraisers as an essential growth area for the next few years.'[86] Similarly, in February 2015, *The Guardian* reported:

> Labour has raised more than £1 million in a Barack Obama-style online fundraising drive that has seen a surge in small donations over the past year. The party has been emailing supporters urging them to donate during that time, with buttons that people can click if they want to donate £5, £10 or £20. Many of these messages are personal in tone, addressing the recipient by their first name, and sent by Ed Miliband or shadow Cabinet members.[87]

Often a person 'donated' money in order to receive a gift from the party, such as a campaign mug, tea towel or T-shirt. In November 2014, the Conservatives sent out an email to their supporters pronouncing 'This is your last chance to order our great "Securing a Better Future" mug in time for Christmas – simply donate £20 today and we'll get it out to you.'[88] In February 2015, Labour sent an email from its General Secretary Iain McNicol announcing: 'We've had them made as *very* limited edition tea towels, and it's your pick: make a donation of £12 or more to get one, or £20 or more for both. (Either way, you'll be helping us kick out the Tories.)'[89]

---

86 See www.conservativehome.com/thetorydiary/2015/06/the-computers-that-crashed-and-the-campaign-that-didnt-the-story-of-the-tory-stealth-operation-that-outwitted-labour.html

87 See http://www.theguardian.com/politics/2015/feb/19/labour-raises-1m-in-obama-style-online-fundraising-drive

88 Email from Conservative Campaign HQ, 12 November 2014

89 Email from Iain McNicol, 26 February 2015

While both these examples are led by national parties, you can introduce similar initiatives for your MP. You could produce mugs promoting significant local achievements by the MP and the party, or design calendars, smartphone cases and T-shirts with the MP's name on. In the US, Hilary Clinton's election shop offers supporters the chance to buy Babygros, a pint glass set and even a 'stitch-by-stitch throw pillow'.

Every MP's website should also have a prominent 'Donate' button on its homepage, as was illustrated by the homepages of the campaign websites for all Labour leadership contenders in the summer of 2015.[90]

Aside from raising more money for the MP, there are two further reasons for doing this. First, someone who makes a donation, no matter how small, is also likely to be persuaded to volunteer during the election campaign – with the right follow-up communication from the MP. Second, should an MP successfully raise a significant amount of money through small donations, you can publicise on their election leaflets and website that they're running a 'grassroots campaign' that is 'powered by normal people like you', which may encourage others to make a small donation if they feel that this is what their neighbours are doing.

HOW TO WORK A GENERAL ELECTION

The regulations produced by the Independent Parliamentary Standards Authority (IPSA) state that staffers are not allowed to engage in political activities during working hours – you are employed strictly to support the parliamentary and constituency activities of the MP. This means that any work you do that is directly related to the general election campaign of your MP, such as organising a

90 These homepages also reinforce the increasing emphasis for websites to collect data from visitors

phone bank, arranging visits to the constituency from celebrities or frontbench members of the party, designing leaflets or door-to-door canvassing, should always be done in spare time and ideally on a personal laptop.

Parliamentary researchers are left in a bit of a no-man's land during the six weeks of a general election, known as the 'short campaign'. When Parliament prorogues, MPs cease to exist – there is no parliament, so there cannot be any MPs – though confusingly the Prime Minister and secretaries of state keep their titles. Your estate pass will be frozen and your office is effectively sealed shut so that no one can enter it. Aside from the decorators and renovators, Parliament becomes a ghost town.

Prorogation is the formal term used for the ending of a parliamentary session, and triggers the official beginning of the general election campaign. To mark the occasion, a ceremony takes place similar to that of the State Opening of Parliament, but in reverse and without the monarch present. Prorogation marks the beginning of the short campaign, as well as the spending restrictions that come into force in order to limit the amount candidates can spend before polling day. During the short campaign in the 2015 general election, candidates could spend £8,700, plus 9p per voter in county constituencies and 6p per voter in borough seats. During the 'long campaign', which begins six months before polling day, a candidate was permitted to spend up to £30,700, plus 9p per voter in county constituencies, and 6p per voter in borough seats.

MPs, or 'MPs standing for re-election' as they become, must place disclaimers on any website or social media accounts to state that they are not currently a Member of Parliament – except on Twitter. The House authorities decided that if MPs were to change their Twitter username, a member of the public might pinch their old one and post misleading or offensive material pretending to be the MP. As well as online spaces, an MP cannot use any printed materials, such as writing paper or leaflets, which have 'MP' on them. In addition, an MP's constituency office cannot be used during the election for any political purposes. Staffers are still allowed to work from it for parliamentary business, but all campaign activity will take place in a dedicated office set up for the election.

The parliamentary authorities have all these rules in place to help level the playing field between MPs and the other candidates. It would, for example, be unfair for the incumbent to use an office with landlines, printers, broadband, paper and envelopes – all paid for through taxpayers' money – to run their re-election campaign. Even the parliamentary email accounts of MPs and their staffers are deactivated.

What, then, does a parliamentary researcher do during a general election campaign? For many it means sleeping in hotels or at the house of their boss or another member of the team for the six weeks of the short campaign in order to work from the constituency office.[91] In the eyes of the public, their MP remains the MP – they, understandably, are not aware of prorogation and the technicalities and regulations that come into effect during the short campaign. Constituents, therefore, will continue to get in touch over the phone, email or social media with casework, or to ask questions regarding the MP's policies. As was demonstrated earlier by the RSPCA's 'Vote for Bob' campaign, many charities and pressure groups increase their efforts during the short campaign to encourage their supporters to lobby their MP (and candidates) to pledge support to their cause in the next parliament.

How much time and energy you put into dealing with this correspondence will depend on your MP. Some MPs will want their offices to carry on responding to everything as normal (even though they cannot use parliamentary letterheads or envelopes at this time – so all the costs for this stationery and postage comes

91 Those staffers who might have grown up in the constituency stay at their parents' home, while some are able to commute to the constituency each day if they work for a London area MP

out of the MP's election fund), while others, who may be comfortable with their majority, certain they're going to lose or just very short on money, might instruct their staff to only respond to correspondence they would consider to be serious and urgent.

If your MP wants you to respond to incoming correspondence as normal, in the course of the six-week short campaign you can expect to draft and send several hundred responses to policy campaigns. Fifteen letters a day will be about average. And, while you will not have the other usual parliamentary tasks of tabling Questions, drafting speeches, attending meetings or giving tours to worry about, you will have many new jobs to keep you busy.

In each constituency across the country, there will be many hustings where one or more candidates take part in a debate. These can be thought of as being semi-professional versions of *Question Time*, and each candidate will attempt to fill the audience with as many of their supporters as possible. Some hustings will be of an open format, where questions on a range of subjects are asked from the floor. Other hustings will be themed; for example, in the 2015 short campaign, the Federation of Small Businesses organised many debates around the issues important to small business, and the National Union of Teachers ran hustings on education policy.

Local businessman Michael Ptootch organised a hustings for his local candidates, which included Green Party leader Natalie Bennett and Labour's hotly tipped Sir Keir Starmer, ahead of the 2015 general election in the garden of his salon and art gallery in the heart of Kentish Town, north London. Ptootch said:

> I wanted to see the candidates in a less formal, more organic environment. Over the last twenty or so years here I've got to know a wide variety of Kentish Town people who are passionate about the community but have little faith in politicians; there was a lot of anti-voting stuff going around at the time and Russell Brand seemed to be reflecting and exacerbating the feeling of disillusionment. This

> hustings was born out of the fact that I'd met a few local candidates and, for the most part, they seem to be well-meaning decent people. I just thought it would be good for regular folk to come along and get close to the candidates and grill them about their plans for our local area. There was a lot of apathy to cut through, but we had a full house of nearly 100 people for our first ever hustings; we broadcast live over the Internet and posted, in full, later on YouTube, where it got a thousand views. This shows that people are prepared to engage in politics if it's offered under the right circumstances. While the setting might have been informal, we were very professional about making this accessible and open to as many members of the area as possible.

Whatever and wherever the hustings is taking place, it will be your job to prepare a briefing document and practise answers with your boss prior to these events. How significant the hustings are will affect how much time you spend preparing for them. If it is a live TV hustings being broadcast across the region, then the MP will spend most of that day going through the briefing document and trying out different variations of their comments. If, however, the hustings is in a small village hall and likely to be attended by only twenty people, then the MP may spend only thirty minutes in the office going through answers and have you verbally brief them during the drive over to the venue.

The process for preparing a briefing document for a hustings is very similar to preparing a speech for an MP to deliver in the House of Commons. Each major party will produce a policy guide (which is basically a longer, more detailed version of the manifesto) for their candidates to use as a basis for being 'on message' with their comments at any hustings, media interviews and online. You can go through this guide, pick out the relevant sections and paste these into the briefing document. Just as you would do for speeches in the Commons, it is best to present this with a structure of 'one issue = one page' to make it quicker for the MP to find the relevant information when up on stage. For an education hustings, this would mean separate pages on class sizes, teacher workload and pay, GCSEs, teaching of sex education, national curriculum and whether or not parents should be able to take their children out of school during term time in order to go on cheaper holidays. Dotted throughout this document should be some snappy attack and rebuttal lines.

Some parties will email all candidates a daily script, setting out their focus and news agenda for the day, while others will issue bulletins every time a significant event in the campaign takes place. During the 2015 general election campaign, after David Cameron's infamous 'pumped-up' speech, Conservative candidates were issued with new guidance that would help them to emphasise how passionate their leader was about being Prime Minister. For Labour, after Ed Miliband hardened his stance on a possible Labour/SNP coalition in the final TV Leader's Debate, the party's candidates were issued with a new script outlining the updated, stronger lines to take in media interviews when asked questions about Nicola Sturgeon. As the person responsible for keeping your MP on message, you need to keep up to speed on all these emails, scripts and bulletins and ensure they are incorporated into their briefing notes, statements to the media and any relevant comments they make on social media.

Finally, you should work with the constituency staffers to complete the briefing document with any specific local issues, statistics or case studies that can highlight the MP's achievements and turn complex, national policy into simple, digestible case studies.

In hustings, as with most speeches and Questions in the House of Commons, being short and sharp is better than going off on a long ramble. Hustings are not a Premiership football match – most of the audience will be close to boredom throughout; a panellist who is clear and concise with their comments is therefore far more likely to be listened to, as well as minimising the risk of being cut off by the chair before they've finished (the ego of the chair is usually proportional to how often they like to cut people off and the length of time they then speak for themselves). For these reasons, it is worth blocking out some time in the candidate's diary ahead of the hustings, even if this is only for thirty minutes, so they can practise answers in front of you and others. In this session you want to challenge their responses, role-play the other candidates and make suggestions of how to improve.

Other tasks you will perform during a general election campaign include arranging visits from frontbench MPs or celebrity supporters of the party. These visits are likely to guarantee (usually positive) coverage in the local newspaper, whose reporters will be grateful for such an eye-catching story. This makes it necessary for you to organise the visit to take place at a photo-friendly and relevant location. A visit from a business spokesman for the party, for example, should take place at a thriving local business, preferably run by a supportive owner who the MP has helped in the past. The story and quotes to accompany the visit will serve to highlight the party's business policies and the image will want to be an action shot of the party's spokesman, the MP and the owner of the business, all ideally in high-visibility jackets and looking seriously at a heavy piece of machinery or the production line. Similarly, if the visit is from the party's spokesperson for families, it makes sense for the visit to take place at a children's centre or nursery.

Just as important as what is in the photo is what isn't in it. One seminal image of the 2010 general election shows two Spads for Gordon Brown lying on the floor in order to hold a door open for the Prime Minister to walk through, leading *The Sun* to run the picture under the headline of 'Flunkies get down on their knees to open a door for Gordon Brown'.[92] The picture became the story

92 See www.thesun.co.uk/sol/homepage/news/2933053/Flunkies-get-down-on-their-knees-to-open-a-door-for-Gordon-Brown.html

of the day, rather than Labour's health-care policies as the party had carefully planned.

The second purpose these visits serve is to rally the party activists, who will be giving up hours of their time to knock on doors, make phone calls and deliver leaflets on behalf of the candidates. Energy and enthusiasm levels naturally drop as the short campaign goes on, so having a significant visitor to give them a pep talk helps to lift the spirits.

• • •

SOME PARLIAMENTARY RESEARCHERS will also be responsible for producing the print and digital materials that go out during the campaign. For print, each party has online templates that allow for text and images to be simply dropped into the relevant box (some also provide suggested 'key messages' on core national issues such as health and the economy). Most print materials are either a four-page newspaper or a folded leaflet. Each will include many, or all, of the following:

- Several photos of the candidate taken across the constituency.
- A slogan.
- The candidate's pledges for the local area.
- Key national party priorities.
- A personal statement from the candidate; perhaps setting out their connections to the area or their record of success as the MP.
- Endorsements from a few residents in the constituency.

- A short survey asking the constituent which party they intend to vote for at the election.

- Contact details, including website address and social media.

Print materials always take longer than expected to complete, and the trick is to start thinking about what the photos need to be months in advance. It can be difficult to find relevant stock photos of your MP that are of a high enough quality and will also reinforce the core messages in the text. This being the case, sometimes it will be necessary for you to send your boss out on a photoshoot across the constituency to collect the necessary images. Any photo that features the face of another person has to be checked with them to make sure they're happy to appear in the publication. Condensing language down into short, sharp sentences takes multiple drafts and, finally, all members of the team need to thoroughly proof-read the entire document before it is sent to the printers. Clearly the team of Samir Jassal, the Conservative general election candidate in East Ham in 2015, forgot this vital last step. The final call to action on Jassal's election leaflet read 'For a strong and effective MP who will be accountable to you, vote Name Surname on 7th May'. Similarly, Labour's candidate for the South Staffordshire constituency could have done with running a spell check through his leaflet after writing 'South Staffordshrie' across the front.

MPs are always in need of stimulating and original content to upload to their social media channels, and it'll be your responsibility to grab photos and suggest infographics when the opportunity arises during the campaign. This can include:

- Selfies with volunteers and activists.

- Photos with supportive constituents, deep in conversation on their doorstep.

- Photos from any organised visits the MP may take part in, such as to a local business, children's centre, school or local landmark.
- Images of posters in windows, or signs in people's gardens.
- Videos of the MP speaking to the camera about a key policy priority; their proudest achievement as the local MP; or a successful and popular campaign they may have been involved in.
- Infographics – such as the number of cases the MP has taken up since being in office, their election pledges or a significant quote about the area.

As mentioned earlier, all of these messages should include an ask for the follower to either share or retweet the post. Occasionally you can change the ask to be 'will you vote for me?' and direct followers to a special page on your MP's website, where they can pledge their vote, sign up to volunteer in the campaign or make a donation.

On top of all this, you should be monitoring the social media accounts of the other candidates (both what they're saying and what people are saying about them), as well as having Google Alerts (or another media monitoring service) set up to send notifications as soon as one of them is mentioned in the local press or hyperlocal blog.

Finally, along with the other members of the MP's team, you will be expected to go out as much as possible on the door-to-door canvassing sessions, which are likely to operate in the morning, afternoon and evening of every day of the short campaign.

• • •

PARLIAMENTARY RESEARCHERS ARE just as important to the MP during the short campaign of a general election as they are in Westminster while the House is sitting. As well as keeping up to date with their policy-lobbying correspondence, their job is to ensure that their boss is on message, well prepared and briefed for hustings and media interviews, as well as to organise visits and photocalls with the press and drive the MP's engagement with their electorate over social media.

Many staffers are integral to the general election campaign and will be there at the count on election night, watching anxiously as the votes come in. For those who see their boss re-elected, it'll be back to work in the Westminster office the next Monday, where things will be back to normal very quickly. One parliamentary researcher says, 'That first day back I had my boss in my ear complaining they couldn't get their Outlook to work.'

For those whose MP is not re-elected, that's it. Game over. You will be given five working days to clear your office of any personal possessions. After this time, your pass ceases to work and your parliamentary email vanishes. You then must decide whether to move on and pursue a career elsewhere, or head to the 'orphanage' and try your luck getting a job with the newly elected batch of MPs.

HOW TO CAMPAIGN – A CHECKLIST

by Callum Hood, senior parliamentary researcher

My own boss of three years, Ian Austin MP, came out of the 2010 general election with a hard-earned majority of just 649. Elections are not won in weeks or even months, but in years of effort on behalf of local people. With five more years of hard work Ian's majority grew to 4,181 in 2015, against a national swing that kept Labour a long way from government.

Here I'm going to set out a checklist you can use to help win your campaigns.

What's the strategy?

If you're working for an MP they will have already won an election and will very likely be planning their next moves. It's your job to understand the underlying strategy, or come up with one if there isn't one already. You need to understand local people, their views and their priorities. You need to listen to them and build a relationship with them.

Here are a couple of questions that make a good starting place. First, whose backing do you need? Your MP ultimately needs the backing of local people, but you should also think about the distinct groups of people whose backing will be crucial. Second, what do you want those people to think? Broadly speaking you will want them to think nice things about your MP, for example that they are hard-working and easy to contact. Ask yourself what you would like each key group to think about your MP – it might be very different depending on who they are and who they usually support.

The details will vary depending on the MP and the constituency, but this should give you the basics of your strategy – who are we speaking to and what are we saying to them? The next step is to build a campaign that delivers the right message to the right people.

Listening

You may have noticed that there's a fashion for all parties to slap a survey on the back of their leaflets. That's because listening is one of the most important qualities that people want MPs and their parties to possess. That alone makes listening an important activity for your campaign, but there's more to it than that. Done properly, listening will help you pick up on the local and national issues that matter most to people. This should help you decide on the campaigns you lead in Parliament and in your constituency.

In turn, this supplies accurate information to help keep your strategy on track. If your key voters are concerned about your MP's local credentials then showing that they're in touch with the local area will have to become more of a priority.

But slapping a survey on the back of your leaflets isn't listening if that's the end of the exercise and you carry on as usual. If you want people to believe that you listen to them, you must actually listen to them – not just say that you do. You have to seek out people's views and then demonstrate that you have acted on them. First, every time someone shares their views you should respond by telling them what you think – just like a conversation. Second, you need to be able to show what you did as a result of having listened to their views, demonstrating what you changed or how you spoke up for them.

Here are a few ways you can make listening part of your campaign:

- Casework: Ensure that people who contact your MP get a timely response, with details of the action that you're taking as a result. That could be a letter to the local council or a government minister on their behalf, with an update when your MP gets a reply.

- Email: Emails enable you to contact lots of local people quickly. You can carry out surveys and update constituents with the action you take as a result. Think about sharing the results of surveys, with videos of your MP taking up the issues in Parliament, or call for further action like signing a petition.

- Social media: Like email, Facebook is useful for engaging a wider audience with listening campaigns and allows for short conversations too. Twitter has a less local audience, but is still useful for reaching figures like community groups and local papers.

- Print: Don't be afraid to produce serious, detailed surveys as they demonstrate a serious attempt to listen. Try to include photos and press cutting in responses to everyone who takes part and in any relevant future material you put out.

- Phone bank: Canvassing can also be done over the phone. Phone banks are particularly useful for reaching harder-to-reach demographics, or those who live far away.

- Community meetings: Community meetings are an excellent way to discuss issues in more detail and can function like an informal focus group. Make sure you collect details from every attendee so that you can send them a follow-up with evidence of action taken.

- Doorsteps: Take a local issue out on the doorstep with a survey or petition and make sure everyone you speak to gets an update on the results. You can do the same by phone too.

The next step is to demonstrate that you have listened by taking action. That's where your MP's work in the community and in Parliament comes in.

Community campaigns

MPs have an authority to pick up local issues and make changes in their area that no-one else does.

In all of your listening activities you should be vigilant for local issues that go beyond casework and affect the wider community. Here are some examples:

- A community group in need of support, for example a football team that needs new facilities.

- A local problem that needs to be tackled, like litter or speeding along a particular road.

- A problem that the whole constituency faces, like attracting shoppers or tackling youth unemployment.

Once you have identified one of these issues there are a number of things that your MP can do:

- Get publicity: MPs get a hearing with local papers, and this can really benefit local community groups or businesses that want local people to hear about them. It can also help gather extra support for any local campaigns that you are running.

- Gather support: MPs have the resources to print a petition or survey and deliver it to local people. A petition or survey with a few hundred backers can make all the difference when trying to get the local council to take action on an issue.

- Get action: An MP's intervention can push local councils, the government or a third party to take action on an issue. The last thing they want is the MP taking the issue into Parliament or onto Twitter.

- Link up: MPs can sometimes make a difference just by putting one group they know in touch with another. For example, an MP can be uniquely placed to put local businesses in touch with a local football team in need of sponsorship.

Make sure you keep in touch with local people who have worked with you on community campaigns. They will often become strong supporters and endorsers of the MP.

Speaking up in Parliament

Constituents don't just expect an MP to make changes locally, they expect them to speak up for them in Parliament too.

Westminster often appears remote to people in the rest of the country, but bringing local concerns to Parliament helps them feel better represented.

You should get a good idea of the top national issues that local people want your MP to speak up on in Parliament from the work you do to listen to local people and the casework you receive. Sometimes it will also be appropriate to take a community campaign to Parliament because there's a national issue at stake in the campaign.

Bringing constituents to Parliament for a visit is also a powerful way of demonstrating that their MP brings them and their views closer to Westminster.

Here are some of the ways you can use Parliament in your campaigns:

- Contact ministers: You can demonstrate that your MP is taking up policy issues raised in casework or surveys by writing to ministers and sharing replies with constituents. Bigger campaigns are also a good opportunity to ask for a meeting with ministers to reflect the seriousness of the issue, for example the closure of a local A&E.

- Organise visits: Arranging for constituents to visit Parliament is a great way of showing that your MP is their direct line to Westminster.

- Present petitions: Presenting a petition is a very effective way of taking a local campaign to Westminster. Wording must be agreed with the Clerk of Petitions but then the presentation can be arranged for the end of any Sitting day.

- Table Questions: Tabling Written or Oral Questions shows that your MP is challenging the government on an issue, and answers can form the basis of follow-up work.

- Debates: Constituents will be impressed that an MP has given a speech on an issue they care about, and the parliament.tv website has now made it much easier to share clips. MPs can also apply for Adjournment or backbench debates to bring local concerns to Westminster.

- Join campaigns: Many parliamentary campaigns are carried out by way of All Party Parliamentary Groups and Early Day Motions. Both are easy to get involved with and can be a good platform for demonstrating action on an issue.

These are just some of the ways in which you can take action on the issues that matter to local people, but the final step is to communicate what you have done.

Communicating it

You need to tell everyone!

Return to those basic questions – who are we talking to and what are we saying? Make sure you're talking to the constituents about all the hard work that you are doing.

That way you can get your boss re-elected and keep your job. More importantly, you can make a real difference by fighting for people who have been let down or by helping the local community. Not many jobs give people the chance to do that!

Chapter 9

The rest

HOW TO DO PARTY CONFERENCE

PARTY CONFERENCE IS a busy, bustling time when the whole of the Westminster Village becomes condensed into one conference venue. TV cameras are everywhere, there's plenty of free alcohol and drinking continues in the hotel bar until the early hours. Damian McBride, Gordon Brown's former spin doctor, calls conference an '18–30s holiday in suits'. Despite them being hard work, you will probably find conference to be one of the highlights of the year.

Conference attracts thousands of people; as well as the politicians, journalists and party supporters there will be huge numbers of businesses, charities and lobbyists who are seeking to showcase their brand, promote their message and meet with senior elected representatives. Dr Matthew Norton, the head of policy and public affairs at Alzheimer's Research UK, explains what this meant in practice for his organisation for the 2014 conference season.

> At Alzheimer's Research UK we use party conferences to take our message to MPs and peers, and particularly those in the ministerial and shadow ministerial teams with responsibility for dementia research – Health and Business.
>
> To do this we held fringe events, which focused on how the future government should support dementia research in the next parliament. The idea behind these sessions was to get the party members and supporters to listen to our vision and ideas and hopefully incorporate them into their thinking and planning for each of the party manifestos that they launch in the run up to the next general election in May 2015.

Planning for party conferences, which tend to last for four days, will begin months in advance. The businesses, charities and lobbyists will start contacting your MP in late May to schedule meetings or to ask them to speak at their fringe event.

Fringe events, or 'the fringe', are the many individual events that take place around the main conference hall, or nearby in a pub or hotel reception room. There are hundreds of these events, with many organisations in attendance hosting a range of debates, seminars, workshops and receptions throughout the conference.

The duties required of you during conference will depend largely on your boss. Some MPs will want their name in the conference guide as much as possible so will accept all their speaking invitations. Other MPs hate conference and don't bother to attend.

As you're likely to be the only member of staff attending with the MP you will take on the majority of the organisation and planning for conference. Your most important task is to ensure they have a suitably full diary. The following steps outline how this can be done.

1 Speak with your MP in early May to discuss how busy they want to be at conference. It's also good to know in advance if there are any organisations they would like to meet, and whether they would like to speak at a fringe event they may be hosting. You can then proactively approach these organisations to ensure your MP gets the meeting or speaking slot they want.

2 For all the other meeting requests and invitations the MP receives – to speak at fringe events, attend receptions and dinners (of which there will be anywhere between 100 to 300) – it's best if you collect all of these together and once a week task the MP to go through them to identify which they want to accept and which they'd rather decline.

3 Arrange fringe events and dinners first as meeting times can be more flexible. For fringe events, it's best to call the organiser to talk through who else has been invited to speak and ask if the debate is likely to focus on any reports the organisation is planning to publish ahead of conference (if so, ask to receive an advance copy of this). Similarly for meetings, it's good to know in advance if there are any specific issues the organisation wants to raise with the MP, and also talk through a good meeting place (there are thousands of people at conference and finding a free table to have coffee can be difficult). For all the invites your MP accepts it's crucial you keep a record of the mobile phone number of someone from the organisation in case there are any last-minute changes to the diary.

4 For the invitations the MP wants to decline, respond to these by email. It's best to send them a quick message to thank them

for the invitation and politely decline, rather than ignore it completely.

Organising the conference diary so far in advance means that it's inevitable things will need to be moved around and rearranged closer to the time. The MP may secure a speaking slot in the main conference auditorium (the most high-profile thing they can do at conference) or may be asked to cover a fringe for another MP who has to drop out.

• • •

CONFERENCE IS A tiring time for parliamentary researchers – with very little opportunity to relax. It can also be very expensive. Unlike the Spads, who will have their accommodation paid for by the party, you will have to cover the cost out of your own pocket. Party conferences are, by their nature, political events, and IPSA – rightly – refuses to allow any expenses to be claimed by those who attend. This extends to MPs, who also have to pay for their ticket, travel and accommodation themselves.

The first step to attending conference is to apply for a pass. This has to be completed several months in advance and will cost close to £100 for a full conference pass. A small saving can be made by supplying a selfie head shot, rather than scanning in a photo taken in the photo booth.

Staffers will then look to group together to split the cost of renting a flat or hotel room (the cheaper the better) and cram it so full that people will be sleeping on any sofa or available floor space. You'll be busy from early in the morning to late at night, so having comfortable accommodation is not a priority. Food and alcohol prices at conference are high, so look to fill up on the freebies offered at the debates and evening receptions you attend with your boss.

It's at conference when you will most accurately earn your label as 'bag carrier'. Your purpose for being there is to ensure the MP is in the right place at the right time. Fringe events will overrun, meetings will need to be rearranged at the last minute and MPs constantly bump into people they know, who will all want to stop for a long chat with them. You need to be tough and not afraid of interrupting this conversation to get your boss where they need to be. You are also responsible for making sure the MP has any necessary speaking notes or background briefings for the fringe events they're participating in.

Here are a few things a parliamentary researcher needs to keep in mind at conference:

- What media/social media opportunities can be created? Despite the significance and importance of party conference to the Westminster Village, the public barely notices. Try to find a way to connect the conference to the constituency, such as making a daily diary for the local newspaper's website or uploading videos, pictures and infographics to the MP's social media.

- Check location of fringe event venues. Some fringe events take place ten to fifteen minutes' walk from the main conference hall. It's important to know this in advance to ensure you're not caught out and your boss doesn't arrive late.

- Make time for security: Getting into the 'ring of steel' (the secure zone that surrounds the main conference area through which only people with passes are allowed) can take a while at busy times. It's always worth allowing for delays when heading into the conference area for a fringe event or meeting.

- Have a phone charger: A sound investment for any staffer before heading off to conference is to buy a portable charger for their phone. Even if your battery is fine, your MP will almost certainly need to recharge their phone having spent much of day refreshing Twitter.

- Try to go to fringes: As well as attending all the necessary engagements with your boss, you are likely to want to attend any fringe events and receptions you have a personal interest in. Some MPs will encourage you to do this, others will want you welded to their side throughout conference.

- Network: With so many organisations and businesses at conference, it is a great opportunity to meet people and make useful contacts at places you may wish to work in the future.

- Pace yourself: Conference lasts for four days, and your boss will require you to work throughout. Don't go too hard on the first night.

HOW TO BE LOBBIED

The premise of the role of lobbying is to persuade. This ranges enormously. Thousands of individuals do this daily by sending their MP emails or tweets on behalf of a charity or pressure group they are motivated by. Professional lobbyists, also known as public affairs professionals, are those who are employed by these organisations – as well individuals who work for a public affairs agency, a business or think tank – and seek to set up the opportunities for their campaigns to be heard in Parliament, and acted on by the government. In the words of Gill Morris, former chair of the Association of Professional Political Consultants (APPC), 'Lobbying and public affairs agencies can help get views and facts across on issues MPs are, or should be, interested in.'

Lobbyists will contact an MP to seek their support for legislative change at a national level. Some will approach you and your boss to discuss a local matter. For example, they may represent a company seeking planning permission to build a new waste incinerator or a shopping mall in the area and want to talk through their plans with the local MP to see if they can gain their support for the project.

In general, you will work with lobbyists for the following purposes:

- Assisting with Questions and amendments: Lobbyists are able to support a parliamentary researcher in determining useful content for a Question, as well as advise on the best way of wording it.

- Providing background briefings and other material: As the case of NDCS shows, lobbyists can provide MPs and parliamentary researchers with briefings ahead of debates.

- Providing assistance to All Party Parliamentary Groups: some charities and think tanks provide a secretariat role to help set the agenda for an APPG alongside its parliamentary members.

In providing you with this support lobbyists can be extremely useful. These individuals and organisations are often experts in their field, and a friendly phone call or coffee in Portcullis House can sometimes be far more productive than days of independent research.

But, while it is useful to call upon their expertise, it is crucial that you should not simply be a puppet to their cause. The 'Insight' investigation by the *Sunday Times* in 2013 caught a lobbyist on film

> boasting that [he] masterminded a House of Lords debate to push a paying client's agenda and fed the opening speech to a peer who read

> it out almost "verbatim"... The lobbyist also said that he could write Parliamentary Questions, motions and amendments that would be put down by politicians who were convinced by his case.[93]

If your MP is discovered to be in the pocket of a lobbyist in this way they will receive huge media attention, which will severely damage their reputation among their constituents. You should seek to use the expertise and experience of lobbyists to help your boss put across their message and campaign on matters of importance to their constituents and constituency, but never just copy and paste their work.

The correct way for public affairs professionals to seek to work with MPs and parliamentary researchers is to be open, cooperative and supportive, but not pushy or controlling. Sarah King, director at public affairs agency Connect Communications, explains below the approach she believes lobbyists should take when seeking to work with you and your MP. In order to work effectively and ethically with lobbyists it is important for you to understand the objectives and tactics they use.

- Invest time in relationships: Parliamentary researchers are invaluable, they understand the interests and priorities of the MPs they work with, often better than anyone else. A lobbyist should take the time to meet you rather than relying on email.

- Be clear and transparent: A lobbyist should be absolutely clear as to which client they are working on behalf of and why they are making contact.

- Tailor research and briefings: A lobbyist should provide information and evidence that backs up their client's arguments and can be used easily by you in speeches and other contributions.

93 See www.thesundaytimes.co.uk/sto/news/insight/article1277757.ece

- Make information relevant: A lobbyist should provide evidence at the constituency level wherever possible. Annual reports and other glossy publications never deliver a good result.

- Make it about people and solutions: You and your MP want to know about the experiences of people, and what can improve public policy.

- Be sensitive to parliamentary and political priorities and pressures: A lobbyist should consider what might be helpful to a new parliamentary researcher working for a new MP, or what is on the mind of an MP and his office in a marginal seat three months from a general election.

- Personalities and relationships: A lobbyist should try to get a sense of how you work with your MP. Each relationship is different, so their dealings with you should be tailored to your needs and ways of working.

- Offer to help: From checking room availability to talking to other parliamentary researchers.

- Finally: A lobbyist shouldn't hassle, even if their client is hassling them.

HOW TO RUN A PARLIAMENTARY OFFICE

It's unlikely that you will have had a job before that caused you to worry about stock levels of paper, pens and envelopes. To suddenly be responsible for monitoring thousands of pounds' worth of stationery supplies can come as a bit of a surprise, and isn't a job many parliamentary researchers do brilliantly well.

Parliament has a relationship with office supply firm Banner. Staffers can order new supplies direct through Banner's website, who will automatically send the invoice to IPSA for billing from the MP's stationery budget. This eradicates the need for you to worry about paying with a credit card or collecting and filing receipts. Banner also supplies the 'official' Houses of Parliament stationery to MPs and Lords – the ivory-coloured, portcullis-embossed envelopes and paper they use for correspondence

Since there are so many other tasks that need doing, taking stock of the amount of paper or envelopes in the office never really makes it up the priority list to be number one. Fortunately, though, when you do run out of things, there are 649 offices on the estate who are all working from the same basic stationery.

HOW TO HANDLE THE POST

All mail is first sent to the sorting office in the basement of Portcullis House. Some MPs will ask the sorting office to bundle up all their post and send it daily to the constituency office. Others will ask for everything to be sent to the parliamentary office, while a few will ask for a hybrid of the two options – with any post looking as though it's from a government department going to the parliamentary office, and the rest going to the constituency.

You will want as much post as possible to be sent to the constituency for the office manager or secretary to sort through. Just as MPs receive gigabytes worth of email, they receive tonnes of post. Sorting the post may take up to half an hour each day – with casework correspondence forwarded to the caseworker, parliamentary and policy documents to the parliamentary researcher, and letters from local bodies going to the office manager. All of this adds up to many hours each month, which you will be grateful to avoid.

HOW TO MAKE A BREW

George Orwell wrote, 'There is also the mysterious social etiquette surrounding the teapot.' In an MP's office, as in most places, be good at making tea and you will go far.

Parliament has all the facilities of a modern office building and there are numerous small kitchenettes dotted across the estate that are open to all to use for making cups of tea and warming up their lunch in the microwave.

More like students' halls than a place in which the nation's laws are made, there is a substantial amount of milk and lunch theft from the fridges in these kitchenettes. In 2012, the *Daily Mail* reported:

> Labour frontbencher Liz Kendall has laid bare her frustration after her packed lunch was stolen in a major breach of communal fridge etiquette. Angered by the thief, she stuck a hilarious handwritten note on the fridge door warning people of the threat posed by the lunchbox burglar.
>
> The note said, 'Someone has stolen my lunch from this fridge. I do not appreciate this and warn other people don't leave anything in here unless you're happy for it to go missing. Liz Kendall, Room 219.'
>
> The culprit, responding on a bright yellow Post-it note, announced, 'I took it ... AND I'D DO IT AGAIN.'

Rather than writing notes, others play dirty. 'Every Thursday someone kept stealing my ham and mustard sandwiches from the fridge that I would lovingly make at home – I think it was an MP who took it for the train ride back to the constituency,' tells one vigilante. 'So I made a special sandwich, with crushed laxatives mixed into the mustard. True to form, next Thursday lunchtime it was gone.'

HOW TO KEEP THE PLACE CLEAN

Cleaners work throughout the night to keep Parliament looking its best. MPs' offices, however, receive rather less attention and are, generally, pretty dark, dingy and dirty places. Some of the oldest offices near the House of Commons have no windows. Ben Bradshaw, MP for Exeter, tweeted: 'Urine seems to be pouring through the ceiling into my Commons office for the second day running!' According to the BBC, Bradshaw's staff used a bucket to collect the drips until the House authorities solved the problem. Pauline Latham MP says staff have walked into her office to find three mice on top of their desk 'pooing and urinating'. Latham claimed to be 'scared to go into my office at night and switch the light on in case they're scurrying away'.[94]

Parliament is full of rodents. On top of the picture rails in the terrace cafeteria are rat-catching boxes, and mice will regularly emerge in the staff bar near closing time to nibble on dropped crisps. Each office receives a fairly perfunctory glance from a vacuum cleaner every few weeks, but in the corners, under the desks and behind the radiators is dust and detritus dating back over many parliaments. The kitchenettes aren't much better. You are responsible for cleaning your mugs and lunchboxes though many choose to just dump them somewhere in the room and leave them to collect mould.

HOW TO MANAGE THE PHONES

Some offices have a 'shit phone'. This will be the phone number that's publicised on the MP's website and parliament.uk. If this phone rings, it will probably be a constituent, a lobbyist or a

94 See http://www.bbc.co.uk/news/uk-politics-26048698

charity. If it's a constituent, you'll enjoy being able to advise the caller to phone the local office. If the call is coming from a '020' number (the London area code), it's likely to be a lobbyist or a charity, probably calling to chase an email they've sent to the MP but you've yet to respond to.

You should give out your mobile number on the signature of your email – not the office landline. You spend a lot of time out of the office and need to be accessible wherever you are.

Some offices will have an answerphone – though many choose not to. Constituents who get through to an answerphone often find that it is full and they're unable to leave a message. Others will discover that the MP's answerphone 'welcome' message is (purposely) so long and dull that they hang up before it finishes.

HOW TO MANAGE AN INTERN

Don't take on an intern simply to give them the jobs you can't be bothered to do. It's not fair on them and it's a missed opportunity for you to learn important management and leadership skills.

It's likely you will lead the interview process as you'll be the intern's line manager. In potential interns, you want to look for someone who has connections with the constituency, or has taken the time to study the MP's interests and demonstrate why they would be a good fit in the office – in short, all the qualities you demonstrated in your application. In the interview, it's important you give a prospective intern a realistic overview of the work they'll be doing. It's unfair to let them think they'll be writing speeches for the House of Commons if they're actually going to spend all their time doing data-inputting. When the selected intern arrives in the office, talk them through what to do, explaining not just how, but why. They will want to know how the task they're performing fits into the wider strategy and priorities of the MP. It's also nice for you to give the intern a tour of the estate when they first arrive so that they can see everything. If you're good at getting PMQ tickets, treat them to a place in the gallery on their first Wednesday. Finally, take them along to the staff bar – an intern should be made to feel a valued part of the team.

HOW TO ENJOY YOUR SOCIAL LIFE INSIDE PARLIAMENT

Many parliamentary researchers feel one of the best aspects about working for an MP is the social side of the role. Being around hundreds of similarly aged people, with Westminster's cheapest alcohol prices available in the staff bar (a pint is around £1.50 cheaper inside Parliament compared to the nearby pubs) and lots of evening events and functions, there are plenty of reasons why so many fall in love with their life inside Parliament.

It's likely you will develop a close support network and friendship group among other staffers – and many of these friendships will last long after you have all left Parliament. The stresses, strains and strange situations staffers frequently experience forges close bonds between individuals.

For a new staffer, though, Westminster can seem a daunting place to meet people. You are likely to be so preoccupied with worrying and learning about how to do the tasks your boss expects of you – and everyone else will look so busy and more knowledgeable – that it may at first feel difficult to strike up conversations. However, you must make the effort to knock on the doors of neighbouring offices and engage with other staffers in order to start building the alliances and friendships that will support you throughout your time in Parliament.

You should make it to the staff bar, the Sports and Social Club (sometimes referred to as the 'Sports and Socialist' by some

Conservatives) as soon as possible. Located next to the bins underneath Central Lobby, 'Sports' is, as Michael White of *The Guardian* says, 'the only bar most voters would recognise as a normal pub, with darts results and welcoming scruffiness'. It is officially a members-only bar (membership costs £5 a year and entitles a person to use the dartboard, pool table and even the nearby rifle range under the House of Lords), although the staff are generally happy to serve anyone. Parliamentary researchers regularly bring in groups of friends who are enticed by the opportunity of being able to say they've drunk inside Parliament, not to mention the cheap beer prices.

Particularly on a Thursday night, after the MPs have packed their bags and headed back to their constituencies, Sports is full of parliamentary researchers swapping stories of the week just gone and sharing gossip on MPs and other staffers. When Sports closes at 11 p.m., many staffers will stagger down Whitehall to the Player's Bar under the arches at Charing Cross, which has a pianist taking requests until 2.30 a.m. in the morning. It is not unheard of for a parliamentary researcher to end up sleeping in their office. Access to Parliament is open twenty-four hours and, with no risk of being caught by your boss, the sofa in the office is an inviting place to rest one's weary head after a particularly long night, and a fry-up from one of the canteens the next morning the ideal kick-start to curing a hangover.

In the summer, Sports quietens down as you and your mates migrate your drinking hangout to the roofs of Parliament. The tables above the House of Commons are the most popular. Here you can take your own alcohol purchased from canteens or the local convenience store and sit in the sunshine looking out over Big Ben and the London skyline.

While most MPs will encourage you to make the most of working in Westminster and to hang out in Sports, some issue orders for how tight-lipped they want you to be. One staffer explains:

> On my first day my boss warned me to be very careful about what I say to other parliamentary researchers. Some MPs try to use their staffers to find out gossip and stories on other MPs and she's keen that I don't give anything away that might lead to anything negative being spread about her.

Other parliamentary researchers are more relaxed about what they say:

> The general opinion of the MP I work for, both in the media and among other staffers, is that he's a bit of a buffoon. He's quite eccentric and people are interested to hear about his latest antics. I can make people laugh with tales of what goes on in our office and the strange situations I find myself in – so why not share these stories?

As well as gossip, Sports is a place where staffers exchange help and advice. As Steven Johnson, author the of book *Where Good Ideas Come From* would say, Sports is home to a 'liquid network', a place where people from different backgrounds, different offices and bosses – who all have different priorities and ways of working – can come together and share ideas. One staffer might tell how their MP has just tabled a series of Written Questions which uncovered lots of useful information that their boss is now going to campaign on locally and use to secure press coverage. Or a parliamentary researcher may be interested in learning about how to improve the MP's website, or want to start using adverts on Facebook to promote a petition they're launching. Somewhere in Sports there is likely to be someone who has first-hand experience of any issue and they will usually be more than happy to pass on words of advice.

MPs occasionally drink in Sports, as was dramatically demonstrated in 2013 when Eric Joyce, who was at the time the Independent MP for Falkirk, got involved in a fight and was later arrested. Formerly a Labour MP, Mr Joyce was thrown out of the party in 2012 after being charged with three counts of common assault following a previous altercation in the Strangers' Bar (the MPs' bar). A year later, Mr Joyce was drinking in Sports when his parliamentary researcher got involved in a dispute with police officers in the smoking area. Mr Joyce went outside to attempt to resolve the argument but, according to *Sunday Times* journalist Tony Grew, Mr Joyce quickly began 'wrestling' with the police. Joyce 'appeared to have one of the officers in an arm lock, he put his arm around the officer's neck, and the other police officer was on top of him. I can vividly remember a policeman's hat rolling on the ground towards me,' Grew added.[95] Minutes later special forces officers stormed into a crowded Sports – which was particularly busy that evening as it was karaoke night – shut it down and sent staffers wandering off to fill the pubs across the Westminster Village. Within seconds, tweets and pictures of the altercation were across the internet.

When most MPs are in Sports they tend to be quite reserved and have a unnerved, 'I-know-I'm not-really-meant-to-be-here' look about them. Most MPs, if they want to have a drink with their parliamentary researcher, prefer to invite them to the Strangers' Bar, which is found through an inconspicuous wooden door along the dining-room corridor.

Parliamentary researchers are also allowed to drink in the Lords Bar, however this is nowhere near as grand as it may sound and looks more like a bar found on the top deck of an English Channel ferry. When the Londonist went on its 'Alternative Pub Crawl' through the Parliament estate, it found that

> with its whitewashed walls, low, brightly lit ceiling and minimal furnishings, the House of Lords bar dazzles like the spot lit pate of a

---

95 http://www.theguardian.com/politics/2013/mar/15/eric-joyce-arrest-mp-police

balding peer. The high wooden tables add to the feeling that you're in an underfunded All Bar One. It's quite at odds with the dusty, fusty old-man's pub we'd expected of the Lords.[96]

• • •

THE PARLIAMENTARY CANTEENS are also a great place for socialising, and they're sorely missed by staffers when they move on to new employment. In total there are a staggering twenty-eight different food outlets inside the parliamentary estate and, similar to the bars, they offer good quality food at exceptionally reasonable prices. A favourite among staffers is the jerk chicken. Served with rice, two portions of veg and a can of Diet Coke, this will leave change from a £5 note. In fact, so popular is this dish that Radio 4 have published the recipe.[97] Prices are even better in the Members' Tea Room, which is only open to MPs and the officers of the Commons. It is also worth noting that MPs can – should they wish to – cut to the front of the queues at the canteens and the coffee shop, though very few do this. The names of MPs who do leapfrog the queues, never say 'thank you' when someone holds a door open for them or have poor lift etiquette (i.e. never holding it for someone rushing to get in) become well known among parliamentary researchers.

One of the first acts of your day will likely be to search the menus on the parliamentary intranet to identify which canteen is offering the best options. Some MPs will like to eat lunch with you, however most of your days will be so busy that you'll take your food back to your desk and eat while catching up on reading the latest posts on the local newspaper's website and blogs,

96 http://londonist.com/2010/03/alternative_pub_crawls_the_houses_0.php

97 See http://downloads.bbc.co.uk/radio4/foodprogramme/houseofcommons_recipe_jerk_chicken_or_pork.pdf

or talking through work over the phone with constituency staff. A lunch hour, you will soon discover, is an occasional luxury.

Throughout the year, there are many after-work events when you can socialise with other staffers and grab a free drink. Your MP will be invited to attend many report launches, awards ceremonies and summer and Christmas receptions, where drinks and canapés will be served.[98] It is not compulsory that you attend these events, however, it's good to go to them in order to network, make new contacts, or just be supportive of your MP.

There are also specific social events for parliamentary researchers. Each party will put on a summer and Christmas event for those who work for their MPs and these events are likely to be attended by a few top politicians from the party, with the leader usually giving a speech about the valuable work parliamentary researchers do. These are usually sponsored by a lobbying firm or a business.

Finally, there are many sports clubs in Parliament, such as running clubs, and football and netball teams, which parliamentary researchers as well as MPs are able to join.

HOW TO FIND YOUR NEXT JOB

According to Paul Flynn MP, 'Secretaries are long-term, while researchers last a few years before they venture into new pastures.' While working for an MP can be a very fulfilling and positive experience, there is a high turnover of staff. Among staffers in Parliament, there is a general consensus that two years is about the right amount of time before they move on to something different. One former parliamentary researcher explains:

98 The most popular receptions, unsurprisingly, are the summer events put on by the Campaign for Real Ale (CAMRA) and the Wine and Spirits Trade Association

> Most of us are paid at the lower end of our salary band, and there's little chance of an increase because the staffing budget is already maxed out. After two years living in London I'd not been able to save up any money, so I looked outside of Parliament for a new job where the salaries were much better.

Another says:

> I loved my time in Parliament, but after a while it does grind you down. You can work really hard preparing a particular project or speech only to have it cancelled at the last minute for reasons out of your control. Most days are a bit of a slog and you're always having to react to the wants and whims of other people – especially your boss. While all of this is part of the thrill and energy of the job and of being in Parliament, after a while I wanted more control of my work and to be in a more relaxed environment.

Parliamentary researchers rarely struggle to find employment when they feel the time is right to move on, or have been forced out by the electorate. Your understanding of the parliamentary process, connections within politics, the media, public affairs, charities, pressure groups and think tanks, as well as detailed knowledge of particular policy areas, all add up to make you an attractive candidate to potential employers.

Dan Garfield, a former parliamentary researcher and now head of external affairs at the Local Government Information Unit think tank, says:

> It may not seem like it at the time, but working in Parliament gives you lots of transferable skills. You learn the basics such as working in or running a small office and all that entails; whether that's answering the phone to irate constituents; preparing briefings with quick and digestible information; or dealing with a potentially prickly boss at close quarters.

Parliamentary researchers go several ways after Parliament, but few leave the Westminster Village. Many will go to an organisation and work 'in-house' as part of their public affairs or communications team, while others will go to a public affairs agency where they can use their knowledge to guide clients through the best way of getting their voices heard by the government and Members of Parliament. Garfield continues:

> For those who choose to go into public affairs, a job in Parliament can provide a solid background. You learn the rhythms of the political year and appreciate the excitement that Westminster generates. While having some knowledge of parliamentary procedure is important, perhaps the most important skill former parliamentary researchers can add to a job in public affairs is how government works and how to influence it.

Other former staffers enter the third sector and work within a charity's policy or campaigns department, where, again, they'll be seeking to push their organisation's objectives up the political agenda. A few, like the *Telegraph*'s senior political correspondent, Kate McCann, may move to the media and use their knowledge and experience to report on Parliament and hold the government to account.

Some parliamentary researchers stay within Parliament, either by moving to work for another MP (usually one who has more potential to rise through the political ranks to become a minister) or going to work for a Cabinet or shadow Cabinet member as a Spad. Many stand for Parliament. Ex-Speaker of the House Betty Boothroyd started her political career as an MP's secretary and current Speaker John Bercow began his life in Westminster as a part-time researcher to Dr Michael Clark MP. As the government's National Career Service website says on its profile page aimed at people interested in becoming an MP, 'You may have an advantage with a background as a researcher or caseworker for an MP.'

Occasionally, a parliamentary researcher will break free from Westminster. Before going into comedy and writing shows such as *The Thick of It* and *Peep Show*, Jesse Armstrong was a parliamentary researcher to former Labour MP Doug Henderson. Owen Jones, author of *Chavs* and *The Establishment*, as well as a frequent commentator in *The Guardian*, worked in Parliament for John McDonnell MP. For Jones, his time inside Parliament revealed a sense of powerlessness of the place. Jones says, 'Ultimately it made me realise true power doesn't rest with Westminster, and the limits of the place encouraged me to try to find other ways to get my beliefs across, which is why I ended up writing instead.'

There are a few things you will want to keep in mind when you're assessing when and where to move on to:

- Plan ahead: You need to start thinking about your next job many months, if not years, in advance. You will want to use events such as APPG meetings, evening receptions and party conferences to build connections with people who work for the organisations you may want to work for in the future – in the Westminster Village, it's as much about who you know as what you know. If you want to plan really far ahead, only apply to work for an MP who is involved in a policy that you want to work in long term.

- Always be nice: Be friendly and professional with other parliamentary researchers, MPs, and all the outside bodies you engage. It may just be that that one of these people will open the door to your next job. The advice of Alex Hilton, a former parliamentary researcher to Linda Perham, is: 'The Westminster Village is a very small world, so don't alienate people on your way up. You need to demonstrate discretion and loyalty.'[99]

99 http://www.theguardian.com/money/2004/oct/25/careers.theguardian2

- Do something extra: As well as getting the basics of being a parliamentary researcher right, push to introduce new ideas to the office, such as learning how to make infographics, putting together a successful e-newsletter or achieving lots of media coverage for your boss. This becomes currency on your CV in future job applications and sets you apart from the hundreds of other former parliamentary researchers.

- Be open with your boss: Again, it's not what you know, it's who you know – and your boss knows a lot of people. A text from an MP can be far more incisive in getting you a meeting with an organisation than the best-written CV or covering letter. Most MPs understand and expect their parliamentary researchers to move on after about two years as they outgrow the salary and the role. Many, grateful for the service you have provided to them, will be more than happy to assist in finding you a good next job. It is also nice for the MP to see their staff move on and be successful.

- Keep in touch: Your insider knowledge is one of your main assets to your new employer. After working hard to build a good network of friends and contacts throughout Parliament, you should put in the effort to keep in touch with them by going back to Sports occasionally. You will often find yourself calling people in Parliament to ask for contact details for other MP's staff, or for insider knowledge about who's planning to table which amendments, or which lobbyists are contacting MPs on a particular campaign, so don't drop everyone as soon as you leave for sunnier climes.

Working inside an MP's parliamentary office is certainly a formative working experience for many who take on the role of parliamentary researcher. As Dan Garfield says, it equips staffers with a huge array of transferable skills. When these are combined with the network of friends and acquaintances you build, the foundations of a successful, productive and fulfilling career will have been laid.

Chapter 10

Improving the role of a parliamentary researcher

THE RISE OF the parliamentary staffer, both in Westminster and the constituency, has been steep. When Sir Robert Rogers, who stepped down as the Clerk of the House of Commons in 2014 after forty years in Parliament, started his career in the Westminster Village, there were only forty parliamentary researchers – now there are nearly 3,000. While this has been a necessity owing to the changes in the role MPs carry out, advances in digital technology and the public's desire for greater accountability, it has come at a significant cost to the taxpayer. The total staff budget for all 650 MPs is now reaching close to £100 million a year.

The staffing system should, therefore, be open to public debate and scrutiny, and there are many parts of it for the electorate to pick fault with. One aspect that diminishes its credibility and public trust is the ability for MPs to put family members on the payroll. The *Daily Telegraph* sums up public opinion of this by saying 'the decision to offer work to family members in their private offices offers a way for MPs to top up their pay'.[100] At the beginning of the 2015 parliament, 129 MPs (or one in five) employed a family member. Discussing this issue in 2013, the TaxPayers' Alliance said:

> Any politician using taxpayers' money to employ a relative must be completely open about who is being paid, how much and for what. And in the light of past abuses, they shouldn't be surprised when their constituents demand more openness if they fail to give a detailed explanation as to how they are spending that cash.

The calls for greater openness over who MPs employ could quite reasonably be extended to cover all appointments. Given the growing role and influence staffers now exert on the parliamentary process, it would be constructive for greater information about them to be published on each MP's website, such as their names, contact details, their role within the office and the main duties they carry out on behalf of their MP. Doing this would disclose no more information than many businesses currently publish on the staff page of their website. This would be a small step towards adding more accountability and awareness of the staffing system, and may lead to a change in public attitude. Those MPs who have a high turnover of staff might think harder about their management and employment practices should they have to update their staff page every other month. Journalists and constituents too will soon pick up on the frequent changing of parliamentary researchers and may ask questions of the MPs.

100 See www.telegraph.co.uk/news/newstopics/mps-expenses/11706561/One-in-four-MPs-employs-a-family-member-the-full-list-revealed.html

Parliament can take bolder and more direct action towards improving the working conditions of parliamentary researchers. The 'harassment hotline' set up by Mr Speaker is a step in the right direction. In the future, employment training for new MPs could be made compulsory and the Houses' HR department could be expanded to provide help and support for staffers.

Improving working conditions in this way might slow the turnover of staff from Parliament to outside organisations. Parliament is, in a sense, a training academy. It takes young ambitious people straight out of university, gives them two years' work experience at the centre of British politics and then turns many of them out to business, lobbying firms, charities, think tanks and pressure groups. Here, they will use the skills they learnt as an insider to influence Parliament from the outside. An ambitious target would be to reverse this sequence, and for Parliament to attract people who have previously held jobs elsewhere and can bring this experience and knowledge in to their role in an MP's Westminster office.

Pay would have to improve to achieve this. People who work in the role are bright and ambitious. While it won't be popular (the public outrage in 2015 over IPSA's plans to increase MP's salary by 11 per cent show this), it is necessary to increase pay for staffers – particularly that of parliamentary researchers who regularly work upwards of sixty-hour weeks, under stressful conditions. The renovation of the Palace of Westminster will cost anywhere between £3 billion and £6 billion. It would be a shame to spend so heavily on the buildings of Parliament, but not invest properly in improving the training and conditions for those who work inside them.

The use of internships and their working conditions cannot be overlooked either. Parliament runs on a small army of unpaid interns. For those seeking a career in politics, having experience of working for an MP is a valuable asset to their CV and many young people are very happy to give up their time to undertake unpaid internships. However, as the recruitment of interns is a matter for individual MPs, many end up doing tasks and working the long hours that would normally deserve remuneration of, at least, the National Minimum Wage. Intern Aware, who have campaigned for the practice of unpaid interns in Parliament to be brought to an end, claim: 'It is damaging for our democracy if the only people starting careers in politics are those who can afford to work for free.'

We should aim to pay the London Living Wage to those who work in Parliament as part of a nine-month placement as part of their university degree. This money could come from contributions from the university, matched by a contribution from the MP's staffing budget. MPs should look to set up partnerships with a local business, or a local further education college, who may be able to provide some financial and training support for a young constituent to work in Parliament. MPs should be able to transfer money from other allowances, such as those for stationery and travel, in order to ensure that an intern can pay their way in London.

For non-London area MPs, the annual Office Costs Expenditure budget is £23,400 (for London area MPs this budget is increased to £26,050). A significant portion of this – about 25 per cent – is taken up with the paper, printing and postage costs of letters. As the government and Parliament gradually adopt a 'digital by default' attitude (i.e. doing as much online as possible), MPs will save thousands each year by responding to policy emails and letters by email.

MPs are still afforded the luxury of claiming for an evening dinner and a taxi home if they have to stay late for votes. Staffers are not afforded this luxury. While the numbers involved in transferring budgets, or stopping the free dinners and taxis, wouldn't be ground-breaking, for each MP it would release several thousands of pounds that could be pumped into the staffing budget. It would probably receive a big thumbs up from the press and the electorate too.

As well as ensuring those on university-led placement schemes get a fair deal, Parliament should try to roll out the Speaker's Parliamentary Placement Scheme and Parliamentary Academy Scheme further. As Kat Thompson, parliamentary researcher to Luciana Berger MP and former intern on the Speaker's Parliamentary Placement Scheme, says, 'I firmly believe that Parliament should reflect the people that it represents and that it can only flourish when it has the experiences of a wide and varied group to draw upon.' The demographic that is dominant in both MPs and parliamentary researchers is middle-class, white males. To the credit of Mr Speaker and the many MPs involved in these schemes, active steps are being taken to rectify this. The Treasury is now injecting money into the Speaker's Scheme, and the business secretary is taking on an apprentice in his parliament office through the Parliamentary Academy Scheme.

The House of Commons should target reaching a point where there is a paid intern or apprentice in every MP's office. Rather than the existence of interns being a politically awkward issue, as it is now and as highlighted by the work of Intern Aware, it should be boasted about, promoted and applauded. This would have a significant cultural impact upon Parliament and serve to improve working conditions for staff. If all interns and apprenticeships had a body outside of their office – such as their university, or the administrators of the Speaker's Scheme or the Parliamentary Academy – with whom they could raise examples of bad behaviour and abuse, it would force certain MPs to keep their tempers in check and stop demanding that staffers carry out personal chores.

Having a long-term, paid intern or apprentice, who permanent staffers can train and hand real responsibility to, will allow better political representation. There will be more time for deeper research ahead of speeches, more piercing use of Questions, more time to care for constituents who visit Parliament and more time to curate online surveys, Q&As and social media posts that seek to build engagement and a genuine dialogue between an MP and their electorate.

A report published in 2013 by the Institute for Public Policy Research (IPPR) commissioned by the then Cabinet minister Francis Maude MP, found that British ministers were under-supported compared to their colleagues in other countries. It said: 'In comparative terms UK ministers have relatively little direct support to draw on to enable them to do their jobs effectively' and recommended that 'there should be a clear and transparent right for each secretary of state to request the appointment of a small number of expert advisers outside of ordinary civil service recruitment processes'.[101] If a similar report were to be commissioned to look at the make-up of an MP's office, it would almost certainly reach very similar conclusions.

• • •

CONSTITUENT'S EXPECTATIONS OF their MP are changing. They expect them to be busy in the local area and, increasingly, put constituency issues ahead of national party demands. Growing numbers of people are taking actions online and seeking to engage with their MP over social media. At the same time, journalists, campaigners and Parliament authorities are pushing MPs to become ever more accountable and transparent. All of this is making the role of the MP more varied and chaotic.

In response, public opinion of MPs and Parliament will go one of two ways; it will either continue on a downward spiral of distrust and apathy, or it will lay solid foundations for the re-creation of belief and hope in our national politics. While it is ultimately the responsibility of MPs to lead the positive efforts of rebuilding the Westminster Village 'brand', all parliamentary staffers have an important role to play.

Currently, as this book has shown, parliamentary researchers

---

101 See www.theguardian.com/politics/2013/jul/10/ministers-new-powers-civil-servants

are trying their best to keep their bosses afloat in the changing demand and pressures on their role. They are writing letters in response to policy-lobbying campaigns, keeping the press updated with stories, generating content for social media, booking constituents on tours, drafting Questions and speeches and supporting MPs to respond to, and improve, government Bills.

For parliamentary researchers however, the systematic problems of a high-pressure workload, long working hours and relatively low salaries mean that most either burn out or leave in search of better money after only two years. This is not in the best interests of Parliament, individual MPs or, ultimately, the constituents they serve.

Chapter 11

Top 10 tips to succeed as a parliamentary researcher

1 Gain experience: Take on an internship or work experience placement to gain that all-important insight into how an MP's office operates.

2 Tailor job applications: Show the MP why you want to work for them and what you can offer to support their campaigns.

3 Make friends: You will rely on the help and support of other staffers throughout your time in Parliament.

4 Build a strong relationship with your boss: Be loyal, work hard, put them first and support them to provide the best service to their constituents.

5 Build a strong relationship with the constituency office: There can't be any gaps in knowledge or responsibilities between the two offices.

6 Plan, deliver and evaluate: You need to always be organised and looking ahead for emerging issues and opportunities that your MP should be involved in. Take the time to evaluate speeches, campaigns, media coverage and digital content to see where improvements can be made in the future.

7 Monitor local news, as well as social media: You want to know what is happening, and who's saying what online, as soon as possible.

8 Keep on top of policy debates and Westminster gossip: Read the news, listen to *Today* and *Today in Westminster* and skim through all your party's frontbench briefings.

9 Make friends with outside organisations: You will rely on them every day and may look to them in the future for your next job.

10 Do something extra: There are thousands of ex-parliamentary researchers around the Westminster Village. What can you do during your time inside Parliament to make your CV stand out?

Resources

A TEMPLATE TOUR SCRIPT

Your personal 'tour script' will develop over time as you learn new facts and figures about Parliament and have experiences that leave you with entertaining stories to share.

What follows is a basis from which you can create your tour script:

1) Meet in Portcullis House

It is often quicker to get through the security at Portcullis House (PCH) than at the main entrance used by members of the public at St Stephen's Gate. Constituents are unlikely to have ever seen inside Portcullis House before and will be fascinated to see the ground floor busy with MPs, parliamentary researchers and lobby reporters. PCH is, according to *The Economist*, 'increasingly the hub of Westminster life: the place to see and be seen'.[102] It is a nice touch for a parliamentary researcher to collect a copy of Hansard and the Order Paper from the PCH Vote Office for each constituent, which they can keep as souvenirs of their visit.

- Portcullis House is home to over 200 MPs and probably the busiest part of the parliamentary estate. MPs will use the tables that occupy much of the ground floor of Portcullis House to hold meetings with businesses, charities, lobbyists and sometimes constituents (meetings with other MPs and lobby reporters tend to be held in private offices or in the Members' Lobby).

- The first floor of PCH is dominated by rooms used for select committee meetings. These are often shown on the TV (the most famous example being when Rupert Murdoch had a pie thrown in his face while he was giving evidence to the Culture, Media and Sport Select Committee). The first floor also features many portraits of MPs – branded an 'expensive vanity project' by critics[103] – including the portrait of Diane Abbott MP (the first black woman to be elected to Parliament) and that of former Chancellor Ken Clarke MP, which cost the public purse £11,750 and £8,000 respectively.

- The second, third, fourth and fifth floors are occupied by MPs' offices, with longer-serving MPs getting the bigger penthouse suites on the fifth floor, or the spacious corner offices with views across the Thames.

- Visible from the entrance of Portcullis House, through the glass

---

102 'Life in Westminster: The Nomads', *The Economist*, 6 June 2015

103 See www.standard.co.uk/news/politics/mps-spend-250000-of-public-money-on-vanity-portraits-9056130.html

doors that lead to the smoking area, is Norman Shaw South. The old New Scotland Yard building is now home to more MPs' offices, with the Leader of the Opposition suite spanning the entire second floor of the building.

- Visitors always enjoy the story behind the fig trees that surround the water feature on the ground floor of PCH. The exotic trees are rented and were imported from Florida in 2001. According to Freedom of Information requests, the bill for rental of the trees and their maintenance is £32,500 a year.

2) Walk through the tunnel under Bridge Street and stand at the base of Big Ben

Constituents will love walking through the tunnel that connects Portcullis House to the Palace of Westminster. At the base of the escalators down from Portcullis House is Parliament's special entrance and exit to Westminster Underground Station. Halfway along the tunnel stand a unicorn and a lion representing the Royal Coat of Arms for the United Kingdom. The tunnel opens up to become a long walkway that forms one of the main routes that MPs take to get into the Commons chamber. At the time of a vote, this walkway becomes a stampede of suits as MPs dash to make it to the lobby within the eight-minute limit.

The first left turn off this walkway leads to the base of Elizabeth Tower, and just beyond, the entrance to the room where the shadow Cabinet meet.

- No one is sure where Big Ben got its name, but the most likely theory is that it is named after Sir Benjamin Hall, a very tall man who held the position of First Commissioner for Works at the time the clock tower was constructed. Another possibility is that Big Ben is named after a famous contemporary prize fighter, Benjamin

Caunt, who was a particular favourite with the builders who constructed the clock tower.

- Big Ben has a large crack in it. The first bell was cracked by Edmund Beckett Denison, later Sir Edmund Beckett, who was the designer of the clock's mechanism (incredibly, Denison was a lawyer by profession and horology and clock-making were merely his hobbies). In search of finding the perfect note, he hit the bell with a much too heavy hammer and cracked it. A second bell was made, only for Denison to do the same. The manufacturers refused to recast the second bell, so instead it was turned 90 degrees and had a square cut out at each end of the crack to prevent it from spreading.

- The famous 'Westminster Chimes' are believed to be set on four notes in 'I Know That My Redeemer Liveth' from Handel's *Messiah*. The chime was originally written for a new clock in Great St Mary's Church in Cambridge.

- Big Ben is the largest and most accurate striking mechanical clock in the world. However, old pennies are placed on, or taken off, the top of the clock's pendulum should it need to be speeded up or slowed down.

- There are 334 steps from the base to Big Ben.

- At the top of the tower is the Ayrton Light that is lit at night whenever either House is sitting after dark.

- One-third of the way up the tower is a cell in which MPs and peers could be detained for various offences within the chambers. It was last used for this purpose in 1880 when an atheist MP refused to take the oath on the Bible.

- Big Ben was never targeting during the Second World War. The Luftwaffe were able to use the reflection of the clock face as a navigational device.

- The total cost of making the clock and bells and installing them in the Elizabeth Tower reached £22,000.

- Apart from occasional stoppages Big Ben has struck ever since it was completed in 1858.

3) Westminster Hall

Just before entering Westminster Hall through its north entrance a parliamentary researcher can offer to take a photo of the constituents. There is an ideal spot where Big Ben and the London Eye will both be in the background. Constituents are allowed to take photos inside Westminster Hall too.

- Westminster Hall is the oldest (and grandest) remaining part of the original Palace of Westminster and one of the most significant buildings in Europe, historically, politically and architecturally.

- The hall has survived fires, floods, death-watch beetles, explosions and world wars. It has been home to law courts and bookstalls and has seen the passing of thirty-four monarchs and the trial of King Charles I.

- The hall has also seen the trials of famous figures from history such as Sir William Wallace, Sir Thomas More, Bishop John Fisher and Guy Fawkes.

- The building of Westminster Hall was first begun by the son of William the Conqueror, William Rufus, in 1097.

- The most impressive aspect of Westminster Hall is its self-supporting hammer-beam roof built over 600 years ago. It is the largest medieval wooden roof north of the Alps – making it one of the largest ancient buildings in Europe with an undivided interior.

- Leather tennis balls have been found up in the roof of the hall and are believed to have belonged to Henry VIII.

- The hall has also been used for the lying-in-state of monarchs and significant parliamentarians such as Sir Winston Churchill.

- During the Great Fire in 1834, saving Westminster Hall was prioritised over all other parts of Parliament. The same priority was given during the Blitz, with other sections of the estate sacrificed in order to create a break to stop the fire from spreading to the hall's roof.

4) St Mary's Chapel

The chapel is not included in the Members' Tours and access is restricted. To gain entry, you must ask a security guard to unlock the entrance. There is meant to be no photography here, but some staffers allow constituents to take photos as long as the flash is off.

- The Chapel of St Mary Undercroft was completed by King Edward I in 1297.

- By the time of the Great Fire of 1834, the chapel had been used as a wine cellar and as stabling for Oliver Cromwell's horses.

- Members of the House of Commons and the House of Lords, and their families, can use the chapel for weddings and christenings.

- The chapel is used regularly by the parliamentary choir for rehearsals.

- At the back of the chapel is a broom cupboard where suffragette Emily Davison (who famously died after stepping out in front of King George V's horse in 1913) hid, illegally, on the night of the 1911 census. To commemorate her act, Tony Benn MP said in the House in 1988: 'I must tell you, Mr Speaker, that I am going to put a plaque in the House. I shall have it made myself and screwed on the door of the broom cupboard in the crypt.'[104] Mr Benn was true to his word and this plaque can be found on the back of the broom cupboard entrance.

- As the plaque says, hiding in the cupboard in this way meant Emily Davison 'was able to record her address, on the night of that census, as being "the House of Commons". Thus making her claim to the same political rights as men.'

- A new use for the chapel appears to be emerging; the body of Margaret Thatcher was kept here the night before her funeral in April 2013. This honour was also given to Tony Benn before his funeral in March 2014.

5) St Stephen's Hall

This space was formerly the site of the royal chapel of St Stephen's, where the former House of Commons sat before the chapel was destroyed by the 1834 fire. Constituents are allowed to take photos inside St Stephen's.

- When Parliament first formed it could be called into being

104 Hansard, Revolutions of 1688–89 (Tercentenary), 7 July 1988

by the King wherever he might happen to be, but as it grew in importance it gradually became established that it should meet regularly in Westminster, with the Commons sitting in St Stephen's.

- It was in St Stephen's that Charles I attempted to arrest five members of the House of Commons for high treason. The MPs, however, had been tipped off about King Charles's plan. They fled through a back exit and were sailing away on the Thames by the time the monarch entered the chamber.

- Brass studs have been placed in the floor to mark the former position of the Speaker's Chair and the Table of the House on which the Despatch Boxes were placed. If the current House of Commons is in use by the MPs, you should get the constituents to stand on these studs as this will allow them to experience how close the Prime Minister and Leader of the Opposition stand opposite each other at the Despatch Box.

- The statue of Viscount Falkland behind the brass studs on the government side of St Stephen's has a crack in the sword blade. This damage was caused when a suffragette, having chained herself to the statue in protest at the lack of votes for women, had to be freed by police smashing through the sword.

6) Central Lobby

This is the midpoint between the House of Commons and the House of Lords and the place where any member of the public can come to request a meeting with their MP.

- Many constituents will recognise Central Lobby because it's the only place in the Palace of Westminster where film crews are allowed to record. The camera wires are always visible under the radiator to the right of the Commons entrance, and most days senior TV news reporters can be seen practising their lines or broadcasting live.

- Above the four doorways in Central Lobby are mosaics depicting the four patron saints of the United Kingdom. The story goes that:
    - St George for England is above the corridor to the Lords because they believe they are better than everyone else.
    - St Andrew for Scotland is above the corridor towards the bars because the Scots enjoy a drink.
    - St David for Wales is above the corridor to the Commons because the Welsh love the sound of their own voice.
    - St Patrick for Northern Ireland is above the exit to St Stephen's because the Irish are unsure about whether they want to stay in Parliament.
- Every day when the House of Commons is sitting, business in the chamber is begun by the Speaker processing from his office (underneath the Speaker's residence), through Central Lobby and into his chair in the chamber. He will be accompanied by the Serjeant-at-arms carrying the Mace as well as by the Speaker's Chaplain, who will lead the five minutes of prayers before business begins. It is during this procession that the security guards famously shout, 'Hats off, Strangers!'[105]

105 'Strangers' is the old-fashioned and traditional name given to visitors to Parliament

7) Members' Lobby

The Members' Lobby is a private space for MPs – and journalists – when the House of Commons is sitting. It is a place where a lot of gossip and plotting takes place. It is also a great space for backbenchers to lobby ministers about particularly important issues in their constituency away from civil servants, Hansard stenographers and the TV cameras.

- Inside the Members' Lobby are four statues portraying former Prime Ministers; David Lloyd George, Winston Churchill, Clement Attlee and Margaret Thatcher. Many MPs chose to rub one of the feet of their favoured Prime Minister before they are sworn into the House.

- There are still small pigeon holes for each MP, but these are now largely redundant due to MPs being able to text and email from the chamber.

- The whips' offices are also based just off the Members' Lobby and at each vote a whip from all the parties will be standing at the entrance of the voting lobbies directing their MPs in the direction they are expected to vote.

8) House of Commons

At the entrance to the Commons are the big wooden doors that get slammed shut in the face of Black Rod during the State Opening of Parliament. This theatrical act reinforces the power of the Commons over the monarchy when it comes to Parliament. After Black Rod has knocked on the doors three times (which over the years has left a large dent in the wood) they are re-opened and is he able to deliver his summons for the Commons to leave the chamber and walk to the Lords to hear the Queen's Speech. Over the past thirty-five years Dennis Skinner MP, aka the 'Beast of Bolsover', has crafted a tradition for himself 'as entrenched as Black Rod's knocking' according to the *New Statesman*.[106] Each year, after Black Rod delivers the summons, Mr Skinner interjects with a short heckle directed at the government.

Tours must follow the 'line of route', which means constituents walk first through the 'No' voting lobby. A vote is called when there is a division in the House; bells will ring across Parliament[107] and the MPs have eight minutes to get to the voting lobbies before their entrances are locked by the doorkeepers. It then takes another twelve minutes to verify the votes and report the result to the House. To speed things up, MPs exit through one of three aisles, depending on the initial letter of their surname, where their names are ticked off as they pass by a clerk. MPs will then either re-enter the House of Commons from behind the Speaker's Chair or head back to their offices or any meeting they were in at the time of the division.

- The Commons chamber was rebuilt after being bombed during the Blitz. It has a simpler, less ornate style compared to much of the rest of the Palace, and especially the House of Lords.

- The size of the chamber and its confrontational design help to make debates more dramatic. When the chamber was being rebuilt, Churchill argued against increasing its size and it has remained having only 427 seats.

106 See www.newstatesman.com/staggers/2014/06/queens-speech-dennis-skinners-greatest-hits-2014-edition

107 Division bells can also be seen in many of the bars and restaurants around Westminster. Before the invention of pagers and mobile phones these establishments installed division bells in order to be able to attract the custom of MPs, who, while waiting for late votes, would pass the time by drinking and dining with guests

- On big set-piece occasions such as PMQs, the Budget and the Autumn Statement, MPs often sit on the steps in between rows, or stand behind the Speaker's Chair. Both these locations have the advantage of being invisible to the Speaker, meaning the MPs can shout and jeer as much as they like without being seen.

- Before deputy speakers existed, it was necessary for the Speaker's Chair to be a commode, with curtains that 'used to be pulled when the Speaker wished to do his duty'. Members would assist the Speaker by knocking on the wood panelling of the benches to drown out any noise. When the Speaker was done, he would open the curtains and the debate would continue.

- Looking down on the floor of the House are four viewing galleries. Above the Speaker's Chair is where the lobby reporters sit. Running along each side above the green benches are the special galleries for members of the House of Lords, personal guests of the Speaker and distinguished visitors. At the other end, opposite the Speaker's Chair, is the public gallery. This now has a thick glass screen to stop members of the audience throwing objects down into the chamber. This, however, didn't stop members of Fathers 4 Justice who, just months after the £600,000 screen was installed in 2014, managed to hit Tony Blair on the shoulder with a condom full of purple powder during PMQs. The campaigners had managed to secure tickets for the special galleries, which is now why MPs must personally sign to state they trust any constituents of theirs who may sit there. The existence of the glass screen is a real shame as it prevents the audience from hearing the natural sound of the House of Commons during debates. Instead, the audience hears the same audio feed as viewers do at home on the TV or radio.

- This audio is captured by the many microphones that hang down from the roof of the chamber. These are very sensitive, designed to capture only the sound of the person who is standing and speaking near them. The benches have loudspeakers, hidden at head height, in their wood panelling so that members can hear each other better. During PMQs, a Prime Minister will often have one eye on the backbencher asking a Question while straining an ear into the speaker behind his seat.

- The government Despatch Box contains both the Authorised and Douay versions of the Bible (for Protestants and Catholics respectively), plus a copy of the Old Testament for Jewish members, a Koran for Muslim members and the register book new MPs sign when they are sworn into the House.

- Both the government and opposition Despatch Boxes are gifts from New Zealand; the Speaker's Chair is a gift from Australia; Canada gave the Table of the House (which the Despatch Boxes sit on). In total, fifty-one members of the Commonwealth donated gifts and materials to help with the rebuilding of the House of Commons after its destruction in the Second World War.

- During debates, members speaking on opposing sides of the chamber are not meant to step over the red lines on the carpet, which are said to equal two swords lengths' distance apart.

- MPs can sit wherever they like on their side of the House and can reserve a place by leaving a 'prayer card' earlier that day in a slot in the bench. Following the 2015 general election the SNP tried to take the seat where Dennis Skinner MP had sat since he was elected in 1970. The 83-year-old had faced many battles for his prime spot before and swiftly masterminded a way to reclaim the seat.

9) House of Lords

From the Commons a tour will walk straight through Central Lobby towards the House of Lords, where furnishings will turn from green to red. Here, the general atmosphere becomes much grander and stuffier.

As with the Commons, tours must follow the 'line of route' which, again, detours through the 'No' voting lobby. At the end of the lobby, rather than turn left into the Lords, you should lead their guests to the right to see the Royal Gallery and the Robing Room. The Royal Gallery is used for important State occasions, often with members of both Houses present. It also contains a copy of the Magna Carta, the Death Warrant of King Charles I and a model of how Parliament looked before the fire of 1834.

The Robing Room is used by the monarch for the State Opening of Parliament. It is in here that the Queen puts on the Imperial State Crown and her ceremonial robes before making her way to the House of Lords[108] to deliver the Queen's Speech.

- The House of Lords is where the three elements of Parliament – Commons, Lords and Sovereign – come together.

- The Lord Chancellor, the equivalent of the Speaker of the House of Commons, sits on the Woolsack. This is believed to have been introduced in the fourteenth century to reflect the economic importance of the wool trade to England. The Lord Chancellor does not need to control or 'referee' debates in the Lords as the Speaker does in the Commons. The noble peers regulate themselves, so there is no need for a high chair looking down on the chamber.

108 Immediately on the right by the entrance to the Robing Room there a very small, subtle door handle which leads to the monarch's private toilet

- On the day of the Queen's Speech, the Queen will sit on her throne, with Prince Philip by her side (though his throne is three centimetres shorter). After Black Rod has returned with members of the House of Commons (who crowd around at the bar of the Lords chamber) she will read the Queen's Speech.

- When the House of Commons was destroyed by bombing in the Second World War, Churchill appropriated the Lords' chamber for use by the MPs. Members of the Lords met in the Robing Room.

- The House of Lords contains cross benches that are perpendicular to the government and opposition benches. The Lords who sit here are not aligned to any political party. The public gallery, which extends around the chamber, has a low, red modesty curtain placed around it. According to the *Financial Times*, this was installed in the 1960s, 'during the mini-skirt era to prevent their Lordships getting distracted by the view'.[109]

10) Roof of the House of Commons

Two floors above the entrance to the public gallery of the House of Commons is a door that leads out onto the chamber's roof. Only passholders are allowed on the roof – though many take friends, family and constituents up there to admire the views across London and of Big Ben opposite.

11) Terrace

The east front of the Palace is 265 metres in length, and is the longest façade of any building in London. It provides great panoramic

109 See www.ft.com/cms/s/2/b5415d12-94b8-11e1-bbod-00144feab49a.html

views across London and catches the sun until the middle of the afternoon. It is, therefore, an ideal place for an MP to sit with constituents for a cup of tea (though the seagulls are a regular nuisance and occasionally leave their droppings on the suits, or in the lunches, of MPs and their guests).

When the MP has to leave, you can walk the constituents out through the access roads underneath Parliament, past the ministerial car park and the entrance to the Speaker's House to the most suitable exit – the main gates if the constituents are heading off to visit the Abbey or the London Eye, or to the Underground if they need to get a train home.

EXAMPLES OF A PRESS RELEASE

'Turn our lights back on,' demands local MP

Rebecca Pilgrim MP has today called on the council to U-turn on its decision to turn off 40 per cent of its streetlights.

The council are switching off the lights between 10 p.m. and 6 a.m. to save £2 million a year. But Ms Pilgrim says switching off streetlights is a threat to public safety.

Rebecca Pilgrim MP said: 'The local authority is wrong to be turning out 40 per cent of the streetlights in our area. This is a dangerous decision that will put both road users and pedestrians at risk. I'm calling on the council to change its mind, listen to the concerns of local people and switch our lights back on.'

Ms Pilgrim will be joining a group of residents for a night walk on Thursday 1 October at 10 p.m. The walk aims to highlight how dark the streets are when the lights are off.

Editor's notes:

- The council made the decision to turn off 40 per cent of

streetlights at a meeting on 23 March earlier this year. Documents setting out their proposed savings can be found here [insert link]

- Attached is an image from earlier this week of Rebecca standing next to one of the streetlights being turned off.

- Reporters are welcome to attend the night walk and Rebecca is available for further comment. Please call me to arrange either of these.

- Rebecca will be posting images and comments on Facebook and Twitter throughout the night walk.

- I can help arrange interviews with residents attending the night walk should this be of interest.

Pilgrim praises Jesse Grayble School

Rebecca Pilgrim MP has today congratulated pupils across the constituency who achieved record grades in their GCSE exams. Overall 70 per cent of pupils in the area achieved A*–C grades, beating the previous record, which was 67 per cent two years ago.

Rebecca Pilgrim MP said: 'It's great news that local pupils have achieved a record number of A*–C grades in their GCSEs this year. We have excellent schools in this area, with excellent teachers who work very hard to support their pupils to achieve their best. I wish all the pupils the very best as they begin the next chapter of their lives.'

Editor's notes:

- The 70 per cent A*–C grade figure has been calculated by adding together the results released by all the schools in the constituency.

- Rebecca is available for further comment. Please call me to arrange this.

AN EXAMPLE OF A MEDIA NOTE

Dear all,

Please find below an overview of Rebecca Pilgrim MP's activities for the next two weeks.

Today – Rebecca has been at Jesse Grayble secondary school this morning to speak to sixth form students about politics and Parliament. Later today there is an important vote in the House on the government's welfare reforms. If the government's proposals go ahead, we believe they will have a big, negative, impact on single-parent families in the constituency and we've already had many people get in touch to raise their concerns. Rebecca will be posting her views on Facebook and Twitter after the outcome of the vote is announced. Please let me know if you would like any additional comment.

Tuesday – Rebecca has a Question on the Order Paper during Health Questions. She is looking to raise the concerns of constituents from the south east of the constituency, many of whom told us in a recent survey we ran in that area, of problems at the local GP practice, including long waiting times and cuts of the nearby bus services.

Wednesday – Rebecca will be bobbing during PMQs and conducting parliamentary business the rest of the day.

Thursday – Rebecca will be seeking to speak during Business of the

House Questions to praise the recent success of Gordon's Bakery, who this week celebrate their 100th anniversary. Later on Thursday Rebecca will visit Gordon's to congratulate the owners on this achievement. Full details of this visit, including a quote from the MP and Gordon's, were issued in a press release last week. We can supply photos after the visit if required.

Friday – Rebecca is conducting help and advice surgeries in the morning. In the afternoon she will be visiting the Dementia Cafe as part of Dementia Week (according to Alzheimer's UK there are 1,452 people in the constituency currently diagnosed with dementia), before meeting with the Chief Executive and Leader of the County Council for one of their bi-monthly catch-ups.

Saturday – Rebecca will be running a canvassing session in the morning before attending the celebrations at the town's spring fayre.

NEXT WEEK

Monday – Rebecca has a morning meeting with the owners of the town shopping centre, followed by a meeting with local fire brigade representatives. Both these meetings are taking place at the constituency office.

Tuesday – Rebecca has a meeting in Westminster with a large internet company to discuss problems with the rollout of superfast broadband across the constituency.

Wednesday – Rebecca will be bobbing during PMQs. We also have thirty-five school children in Parliament for a tour and Q&A session.

Thursday – Rebecca will take part in Business Questions. We'll decide closer to the time what issue she raises.

Friday – Rebecca is visiting a local logistical firm who have recently announced £1.5 million investment in their operations. This will be followed by a visit to a local children's centre to talk to parents about childcare services. In the evening Rebecca is speaking at a meeting of the local business forum where they'll be discussing transport, broadband, skills training and the shopping centre.

Saturday – Rebecca will be running a canvassing session in the morning.

As always, feel free to give me a call to discuss any of these events in greater detail and follow Rebecca daily on Facebook and Twitter to check for any unexpected news.

A TEMPLATE PHONE-BANK SCRIPT

including a survey question on health issues

Hello, I'm calling on behalf of Rebecca Pilgrim. Can I please speak to [ELECTORS NAME]?

Rebecca wants to learn the views of residents of [NAME OF CONSTITUENCY/ CITY/ TOWN/VILLAGE] about their experiences with local health services. Would you mind if I asked you a few quick questions? (If elector says no, thank them for their time and end the call.)

How well would you rate the provision of health services locally? Good, bad or don't know?

How often do you use your local GP?

Are there any specific issues you would like to raise with Rebecca about local health services?

Thank you for those answers – that's really useful information. Do you mind me asking which political party you would support if there was a general election tomorrow?

And thinking back to the last general election, which party did you vote for then?

That's great – thank you very much for speaking to me, I really appreciate your time and I will pass your views on to Rebecca. Have a good day.

Acknowledgements

I WOULD FIRSTLY LIKE to thank Iain Dale, Olivia Beattie, Victoria Godden and the rest of the team at Biteback Publishing for their support throughout this project. I went into the Biteback offices the Friday afternoon after election night. I'd only had two hours' sleep, and was pretty miserable about the result in Corby and across the country. Talking through the plan for this book with Olivia, and seeing how it falls into a series with their other titles such as *How to Be an MP* and *How to Be a Minister* was a great help.

This book benefits from the ideas, experience and expertise of many individuals. I am honoured that Mr Speaker, Rt Hon. John Bercow MP, has provided the foreword. I think his contribution underlines the important role parliamentary researchers play in the House of Commons.

I want to thank Grace Wright, Callum Hood and Emma Darkins for their contributions. All three were parliamentary researchers at the same time I was. As well as being good friends, they are also three of the most talented staffers in Parliament. The same praise goes to Beth Miller, Russell Antram, Kat Thompson and Vincent Torr (whom I had the pleasure of working with when he joined Andy Sawford's office as an intern on the Speaker's Parliamentary Placement Scheme). I also want to thank the many current and former parliamentary researchers who spoke to me off the record. Understandably, they wanted to be careful about what went into print, but their contributions help to highlight some of the more difficult aspects of working for an MP.

I am also grateful to many people who work elsewhere in the Westminster Village especially Kate McCann, a rising lobby reporter, and Emma Hutchinson, a brilliant regional TV reporter. Elsewhere, I want to thank Kevin Hollinrake MP, Gavin Shuker MP, Steve Hatch at Facebook, Toni Cowan-Brown at NationBuilder, Tom Bage at Change.org, Gill Morris and Sarah King from Connect Communications, Max Freedman at the Unite parliamentary branch, Harry Cole at Order-order.com, Dan Garfield at the Local Government Information Unit and writer and commentator Owen Jones. They all took the time to speak with me and share their insights on the record. I also want to thank the other MPs and members of the Westminster Village who provided off-the-record comments and ideas.

Of course, this book only exists because I worked for a brilliant boss and a brilliant MP and I am endlessly grateful for all the support and guidance Andy has given me over recent years. Andy also employed four brilliant members of staff in the constituency – Lynsey, Alan, Colleen and Ian. All were exceptional at their jobs, loyal and dedicated to the team. I learnt a great deal from them and I am proud of what we achieved together in such a short period of time.

Finally, on a personal note, I want to thank my mum and dad, Claire and John, for their support and for reading numerous drafts. Thanks, too, to Joe for being my buddy at the British Library.

Above all else, I want to thank Myra and Charly.

Bibliography

Carswell MP, Douglas, *The end of politics and the birth of iDemocracy*, Biteback Publishing, 2012

Flynn MP, Paul, *How to Be an MP*, Biteback Publishing, 2012

Hutton, John and Lewis, Leigh, *How to Be a Minister*, Biteback Publishing, 2014

Mattinson, Deborah, *Talking to a Brick Wall*, Biteback Publishing, 2011

McBride, Damian, *Omnirambles*, Biteback Publishing, 2014

Plouffe, David, *The Audacity to Win*, Viking/The Penguin Group, 2009

Rogers, Robert and Walters, Rhodri, *How Parliament Works*, 6th edition, Routledge, 2006